T0354649

The Thistle and the Rose

Romance, Railroads, and Big Oil
in Revolutionary Mexico

Catherine Nixon Cooke

iUniverse, Inc.
Bloomington

The Thistle and the Rose
Romance, Railroads, and Big Oil in Revolutionary Mexico

Copyright © 2010, 2013 John George McNab and Laura Helen Moore Brusenhan

All rights reserved. No part of this book may be used or reproduced by any means, graphic, electronic, or mechanical, including photocopying, recording, taping or by any information storage retrieval system without the written permission of the publisher except in the case of brief quotations embodied in critical articles and reviews.

Map of Mexico (inside cover) courtesy of David Rumsey Map Collection/Cartography Associates

iUniverse books may be ordered through booksellers or by contacting:

iUniverse
1663 Liberty Drive
Bloomington, IN 47403
www.iuniverse.com
1-800-Authors (1-800-288-4677)

Because of the dynamic nature of the Internet, any web addresses or links contained in this book may have changed since publication and may no longer be valid. The views expressed in this work are solely those of the author and do not necessarily reflect the views of the publisher, and the publisher hereby disclaims any responsibility for them.

Any people depicted in stock imagery provided by Thinkstock are models, and such images are being used for illustrative purposes only.

Certain stock imagery © Thinkstock.

ISBN: 978-1-4759-6515-5 (sc)
ISBN: 978-1-4759-6516-2 (hc)
ISBN: 978-1-4759-6517-9 (e)

Library of Congress Control Number: 2012922928

Printed in the United States of America

iUniverse rev. date: 1/8/2013

To our families, we dedicate this book.
May we be ever mindful of the ties that bind us to one another
through all generations—past, present, and future.

Laura Helen Moore Brusenhan
John George "Sandy" McNab

Grandchildren of John George and Guadalupe McNab

Contents

Preface

On a cool September day in 2000, ninety-two-year-old Estella McNab Moore telephoned her nephew, Sandy McNab, to tell him she had something important that she wanted to give him. When he arrived at her house, she reminded him that her father—Sandy's grandfather—had lived in Mexico and worked for the legendary Sir Weetman Pearson's Petróleo El Aguila in the early 1900s. Because Sandy was now in the oil business himself, she wanted him to have several large cardboard boxes filled with black-and-white photographs from those historic times of booming production and revolution. She told him that she had given similar boxes of more personal family photographs to her daughter, Laura Helen Brusenhan, and that she hoped the cousins would sort through them someday. Sandy thanked her and took his boxes to his office, not quite sure when he would have time to look at them.

When Estella McNab Moore died in March 2001, Sandy remembered the boxes, which he had placed in a closet in his office. During the months that followed he got them out, sorted through hundreds of photos, and was amazed at the images of railroad and port construction, oil drilling, revolutionary violence, and ancestors about whom he knew very little.

Not long after the photographs had taken over every table and desk in Sandy's office, a chance lunch meeting served as still another catalyst for discovery. When Joseph Dial, a former director of the Texas State Film Commission, arrived for lunch, he asked to look at the photos. Soon his eyes focused on the image of a remarkably beautiful woman in a white lace dress—Sandy's grandmother, Guadalupe Fuentes Nivon

McNab. "Who is this?" he wanted to know. "What was her family background? There's a story here!"

Sandy told Dial that his first cousin, Laura Helen Moore Brusenhan, had additional photographs, as well as tape-recorded oral history interviews with her mother, Estella, who had been born in Oaxaca in 1907. Dial expressed a desire to hear more of the story, and Sandy promised to contact Laura.

Several weeks later, Sandy McNab, Laura Brusenhan, and Joseph Dial met again. The meeting also included Richard Reed, chair of the Anthropology Department at Trinity University, who suggested they contact Teresa Van Hoy, a researcher working at the University of Houston, specializing in Mexican history. When Sandy telephoned Van Hoy, he told her about the photographs and shared the sparse information he had. She replied, "I have a film of your grandfather at the opening of the Port of Veracruz!"

And at that moment, Sandy McNab and Laura Brusenhan embarked on a journey into the past—a journey that would uncover their family saga and a love story set against the turbulent times of the Mexican Revolution.

Many of us dream of embarking on similar journeys of discovery. As little children, we begin to piece together the puzzle of who we are. Starting with our closest caretakers—whether mothers, fathers, grandparents, or others—we claim them with fierce possessiveness. We are curious about the important people who feed us, bathe us, and rock us to sleep, and simple stories about their pasts intrigue and delight us.

By the time we reach adulthood, we understand that our family tapestry is remarkably intricate, that it includes many characters and stretches further back in time than we had imagined. Eventually, as life's experiences challenge us and shape us, we recognize that those rich stories from our ancestral pasts have contributed to who we are. Sometimes they come as whispered, shadowy dreams; sometimes they are vibrant memories in search of context. Repositories of information like Ancestry.com and Archives.com can confirm or negate vague recollections and provide real data about our pasts; and there is often a "family archivist" who has kept scrapbooks, letters, diaries, and old stories alive. Sometimes these journeys into the past serve to reunite family members who have lost touch; sometimes they solve unanswered mysteries from the past, and they always include a few surprises.

The Thistle and the Rose is the result of just such a quest. It is an epic story of adventure, courage, enterprise, and incredible romance; and it was my real privilege to "live with" the family's remarkable characters for the past two years. The hero, John George McNab, is intelligent, brave, and dashingly handsome—all documented by original records that describe his childhood in Scotland, his immigration to the United States and then Mexico, and the dangers and opportunities of Mexico's revolution, and by photographs that reveal his striking good looks.

The heroine, Guadalupe Fuentes Nivon, is breathtakingly beautiful, and similar documents and photographs confirm her family roots in France and ancient Oaxaca, the Mexican state known for its strong, entrepreneurial women and its wild, lush landscape. The book's title was suggested by Sandy McNab, meant to capture the pairing of a hearty Scottish "thistle" and a gorgeous Mexican "rose."

The story begins in Europe in the early 1800s and moves to Mexico and the dramatic years of Porfirio Díaz that eventually brought revolution to a culturally rich, complex country. McNab was employed by the largest engineering and construction firm in the world, London-based S. Pearson & Son, and he played a major role in the development of the famous Tehuantepec railroad in the early 1900s, and in the discovery of big oil in Mexico in 1910. Both endeavors resulted in adventures and political intrigue the family never dreamed it would face, including a terrifying encounter with the famous bandit-general Pancho Villa, documented by an original letter from him dated March 1911, that is included in this book.

The dramatic escape of a member of Mexico's former royal family to the United States is told in a never-before-published letter that I found in the extraordinary Pearson Archive, located in the Science Museum Library in the village of Wroughton, in the United Kingdom. And photographs—some beautiful and some horrific—as well as original papers from family members and friends, contrast the colorful celebrations of saints' days, *quinceañeras*, and weddings with the terrible violence of revolution, all important parts of the story's backdrop.

Realizing that the first edition of the book would be read by a predominantly English-speaking audience, I did not use the Spanish system of nomenclature; and there is a family tree at the end of the book for additional clarity. At times, specific details of known events were not available, and I took some "poetic license," using information and descriptions of similar events of the times that were documented in various archives and publications.

I was fortunate to have excellent source material for this book, including a research manuscript by Latin American scholar Teresa Van Hoy, and books published in Mexico in the 1800s, now collectors' items. In addition, old church records, census documents, and photographs, diaries, and letters that had been passed down for generations provided a factual backbone for the story. I collected family surveys from McNab descendants across the country, rich with anecdotal material, and I journeyed to the valley of La Dróme to explore the French connection, to snowy England to acquire papers and photographs from the Pearson Archive, and to southern Oaxaca to experience a landscape and culture that hasn't changed much in the last hundred years. I met many fascinating characters along the way; they helped me piece together the details of the story, and all are mentioned in the acknowledgments.

Just as the book was going to press, we discovered a niece of Guadalupe Nivon McNab—Millicent Antelma Gertrudis Craigie Keck—just a few months short of her ninety-third birthday, thanks to Ancestry.com. She was living in Savannah, Georgia; her photos of the Nivon family ranch in Oaxaca, and firsthand stories added important new details at the last minute, proving the power of twenty-first century information networks.

Like Mexico itself, the McNab family is a rich mix of cultures—French, Scottish, Zapotec—and *The Thistle and the Rose* captures that complexity, providing a unique lens through which we can view a magnificent, complicated country during critical years of change.

The story of John George McNab and Guadalupe Fuentes Nivon McNab may inspire readers to explore their own family sagas, set against their own unique backgrounds, peopled by characters that have influenced their descendants in important ways. To embark on the journey one must become an explorer—curious, open-minded about the unknown, embracing the mysteries that are encountered along the way. Our discoveries, sometimes surprising, can provide us with those essential clues that lead us to our origins and the source of who we are.

Catherine Nixon Cooke

Acknowledgments

I love stories about extraordinary people who have embraced life with daring, creativity, and courage. In 2007, Laura Helen Moore Brusenhan and John George "Sandy" McNab shared some highlights of a research manuscript they had commissioned; and it contained elements of just such a story. I was captivated.

Teresa Van Hoy, PhD, a research historian who teaches at St. Mary's University in San Antonio, Texas, had been commissioned to gather information about a family with origins in Scotland, France, and Mexico, whose adventures moved from highland moors to lush jungles, from ancestral castles to haciendas, and from early commerce and industry through the Mexican Revolution.

The hero, John George McNab, was dashing, intelligent, and determined—a skilled engineer who worked for the British firm of S. Pearson & Son, supervising the construction of Mexico's legendary Tehuantepec Railroad, and the field operations of Petróleo El Aguila, the country's largest oil venture. The heroine, María Guadalupe Fuentes Nivon, was incredibly beautiful, with deep roots in ancient Mexico, born on the same day as her country's patron saint. Van Hoy's research manuscript contained critical information and data that gave me an exciting starting point.

Joseph Dial, a former director of the Texas Film Commission, had encouraged documenting the story, sure that it contained all the drama needed for a great film; and during a serendipitous lunch meeting that focused on a totally different project, Dial and another of my most creative friends, Pete Selig, suggested to Sandy McNab that I should join the evolving "project team" to write the book.

Incredible historic photographs from the family's scrapbooks offered still another unique glimpse into the fascinating, dangerous years of the Mexican Revolution. The images in the McNab/Brusenhan family collection are riveting—ranging from the breathtakingly beautiful portraits of Guadalupe to the horrific glimpses of corpses hanging from trees during the violence of revolution. Ansen Seale did a masterful job restoring them, and Crystal Hollis, also a part of Seale Studios, put them into the wonderful graphic design of each chapter.

Through surveys and interviews with family members, including Laura Helen Moore Brusenhan, Sandy McNab, Estella McNab Moore (conducted and recorded by her daughter, Laura, in San Antonio, in 2001), Easton McNab Crawford, Joan Gropper Crawford Mattson, Mary Isabel "Ibby" Crawford, Judith "Judy" Virginia Grafius Griffith, Elizabeth "Betty" Isabel Grafius Moore, Margaret "Maggie" McNab Boerner, Alejandro Nivon, and Gabriela Nivon Malo, I learned even more about the characters in this story.

Additional assistance came from friends like David Rocha, who lent me rare source materials including Travels in Mexico (published in 1880), Picturesque Mexico (published in 1897), and El General Porfirio Díaz (published in 1902); Raúl Rodríguez, former director of North American Development Bank, who read my manuscript for accuracy and introduced me to important contacts in Tampico and Oaxaca; Enrique Krauze, author of Mexico: Biography of Power, who provided important information about land acquisitions in Oaxaca in the mid-1800s; Claudia Rodriguez, who helped translate some of the more formal source documents; and Eva Gonda de Garza Laguera, whose friendship made possible "connections" that enriched the story.

Ricardo and Cheri Longoria, and Shirley Fleishman Grossman shared wonderful anecdotes about Tampico during its "glory days" of oil production in the early twentieth century, and internationally renowned dye-maker and weaver Bulamaro Perez Mendoza, based in Teotitlán,

Oaxaca, explained—and demonstrated in perfect detail—the natural dye industry that played such an important role in Guadalupe Fuentes Nivon McNab's early life in Oaxaca. William Scanlan III introduced me to his friend Constantino Jimenez, a marvelous translator and amateur historian. "Tino" was my driver over the Sierra Madre mountains, rounding curves on single-lane highways from Oaxaca City to the village of Tapanatepec in the far south of the state, where I met Arnoldo Nivon Langner, great-nephew of Guadalupe Nivon McNab, who shared details about the effects of modernization and politics on the hacendado system, and more personally, the Nivon family, in the last decades of the nineteenth century.

A trip in February 2009 to the Pearson Archive, located in the Science Museum Library in the village of Wroughton, England, yielded a treasure trove of letters, photographs, and information about the engineering firm S. Pearson & Son, responsible for building so much of Mexico's infrastructure in the early twentieth century. Some of the documents contained remarkable—never before published—information about the behind-the-scenes politics of the Mexican Revolution. Cate Watson was especially helpful as I examined the hundreds of files pertaining to the company's work in Mexico, including construction of the Gran Canal in Mexico City, the port of Veracruz, and the Tehuantepec Railroad, and establishment of the huge oil enterprise El Aguila, which eventually was sold to Royal Dutch Shell in 1919 for what would be more than a billion US dollars today.

Well-known British author Rosalind Miles and military historian Robin Cross provided detail about Scottish life and military service prior to the McNab family's emigration to the New World, and photographer/ anthropologist George O. Jackson Jr. shared similar background about ancient traditions in Mexico, as well as allowing some of his award-winning images from his exhibit at the Smithsonian Institution—of ceremonies honoring Mexico's patron saint, la Virgen de Guadalupe, for whom Guadalupe Fuentes Nivon McNab was named—to be published in this book.

Sister Mary Magdalen Hanel, archivist for the Dominican Sisters of Houston, shared the history of the order that established the Sacred Heart Academy in Galveston, Texas, where John George and Guadalupe McNab sent their oldest daughters during the worst years of the Mexican Revolution, even finding a composition book that had belonged to fourteen-year-old Estella McNab. While the girls were avoiding the turmoils in Mexico, they experienced a different sort of terror when a hurricane hit Galveston. Richard "Dick" Dickerson, university archivist at the University of Houston Libraries, helped me find vivid photographs of the havoc caused by this famous storm in 1915.

Then, toward the very end of the project, as the manuscript's copyediting was being completed, Joan Mattson had a "hit" from an inquiry about her Nivon family tree that she had posted on Ancestry.com more than a year ago. Katherine Millicent Cornell, from Chattanooga, Tennessee, replied that her grandmother was the daughter of Josefina Nivon, an older sister of Guadalupe. Millicent Antelma Gertrudis Craigie Keck was living in Savannah, Georgia, about to celebrate her ninety-third birthday, and she was a veritable font of historic information and dates, childhood memories of early Mexico, and historic photographs. I flew to Savannah and spent a delightful day with a remarkable woman, recognizing that the truly amazing research aspects of twenty-first century technology had enabled me to add more rich details to an already incredible story.

After a small first edition printing in 2010, the McNab family and I were delighted to discover the wonderful publishing capabilities of IUniverse. Special thanks to Sarah Disbrow and the team of editors and reviewers there for helping us bring this beautiful second edition to the reading public.

And finally, I am so grateful for the constant support and encouragement of my husband, Geary Atherton, during the entirety of this project—his willingness to enter the world of the Fuentes/Nivon/McNab family with me, to drive that long, curving road to southernmost

Oaxaca, and his delight at the treasures we encountered along the way that added richness to an already magnificent adventure.

Catherine Nixon Cooke
San Antonio, Texas

"John George McNab was courageous and sturdy like the hearty thistles in his native Scotland. Guadalupe Fuentes Nivon was both tender and independent, like the red roses she grew in her gardens in Mexico and Texas in honor of her patron saint."

McNab family saying

Prologue

Message from the Heavens

San Antonio, Texas: 1957

After adjusting the telescope carefully, John George McNab straightened up slowly, pausing to rub his lower back, refusing to bow to old age. He stood tall, and his blue eyes twinkled as he called for his grandson and namesake, now six years old.

The boy bounded into the patio and smiled at his grandfather. The sandy brown hair, bright blue eyes, and famous McNab chin proved the power of genetics, and the young boy's curiosity about the flashing comet that lit the night skies during the spring of 1957 reminded the old man of himself nearly seven decades ago.

Together they studied the bright tail of the Arend-Roland Comet, first seen in France in 1956 and brightening so much by the following year that it was known as the Great Comet of 1957. McNab explained the difference between comets, meteors, and stars, and promised his avid pupil that he would show him some wonderful pictures in his well-stocked library the next morning.

Suddenly his eyes misted as he thought about another comet that had raced across the world's skies long ago, when McNab was a young man seeking his fortune in a faraway land. That comet had been a harbinger of change for McNab, the start of his life in turn-of-the-century Mexico, where he witnessed a revolution, built a railroad, helped bring in the second largest oil well in the world, and most important, found the love of his life.

Sensing a story, little "Sandy" McNab placed his hand in his grandfather's and waited for the family's patriarch to begin.

"My grandmother told me that when her sister Guadalupe walked into the ballroom, she recieved 'aplausos'—applause—although she was not the honoree. She was the tallest daughter, with thich chesnut brown hair that fell beneath her knees when it was not in its coil. She had huge dark eyes that flashed with humor and intelligence. More than a hundred years ago, Guadalupe Fuentes Nivon was the most beautiful girl on the isthmus."

Arnoldo Nivon Langner
Great-nephew of Guadalupe Fuentes Nivon McNab

Chapter 1

A Fiery Start

Mexico: 1900s

As the first decade of the new century drew to a close, smoke and ashes filled the Mexican sky for days. Peasants in the countryside agreed that the eruption of Mount Colima in 1909 was a sign that the powerful "Old Ones" would soon sweep the wicked away. A year later, a fiery glare streaked across the heavens. Newspapers described the phenomenon of Halley's Comet in scientific terms, but in remote villages without newspapers, elders announced that the showers of fire were another sign, an omen, a prediction of change and trouble.

The volcanic eruption of Mount Colima was perceived as an omen of trouble smoldering in Mexico. (Photo source: Brown Brothers)

Meanwhile, in the nation's capital, glorious progress was being reported. President Porfirio Díaz, now eighty years old, had just modernized the city with a hospital, jail, and insane asylum, and a spectacular glass curtain designed by the American artist Louis Comfort Tiffany graced the new Italian marble opera house. The international relationships he had spent more than a decade developing now illustrated to the world that Mexico was a land of promise, where men of imagination and money could fulfill their dreams. And men, money, and dreams were streaming in.

President Porfirio Díaz brought modernization to Mexico, but his thirty-year term ended in revolution. (Photo source: General Bernardo Reyes, *El General Porfirio Díaz*, J. Ballesca y Compañía, México, 1903.)

American funds had absorbed plantations and ranches—rich in cotton, sugar, timber, and cattle—and holdings were estimated at $500 million by 1902, surpassing the Spanish-owned lands, which had been the largest for generations. A German financier named Hugo Scherer directed large amounts of European capital to Mexico through government loans, and President Díaz was negotiating with Japan for payment in exchange for huge concessions in Baja California. The London-based engineering firm S. Pearson & Son had built the *Gran Canal* to control flooding in Mexico City, dredged a new port for Veracruz, was building the Tehuantepec Railway across the strategic isthmus, and was drilling for oil in partnership with the Mexican government as the El Aguila Oil Company.

At the turn of the century, as *Tata Porfirio* celebrated his eightieth birthday in 1902, a modern hospital (above) and marble opera house were built in Mexico City. (Photo source: General Bernardo Reyes, *El General Porfirio Díaz*, J. Ballesca y Compañía, México, 1903.)

Its chairman, Weetman Pearson, was rewarded at home for his extraordinary international success when he received the title of baron from His Majesty's Government in 1910. He adopted the name of his vast estate in Sussex for his title, becoming Lord Cowdray. Still later in his career, he would be named first Viscount Cowdray, an even bigger honor in the British world of titles. Meanwhile, as Pearson was expanding his operations around the world, his employees in Mexico were hearing the first rumblings that the world of *Tata Porfirio* and *Doña Carmelita* would end with the elections in 1910. They joined other foreign operators in their concern that an intellectual young man from a wealthy northern family was talking about the presidential succession, the Constitution, and giving Mexico's land back to the poor. Francisco Madero was a man to worry about; he seemed to confirm the comet's fiery message that change was ahead.

British entrepreneurs Sir Weetman Pearson and Lord Aberdeen recognized the extraordinary opportunities for financial gain in Mexico as the nineteenth century came to a close. (Photo source: Brown Brothers.)

The last decade had seen a boom in the Pearson operations, and a handsome young Scotsman named John George McNab had signed on as an engineer in 1896, determined to make his fortune in a new land of opportunity and adventure. The rumblings of change had not yet begun, and on a beautiful Saturday afternoon in Veracruz, in 1898, McNab was looking forward to the diversion of a *quinceañera* ball after several long weeks of surveying work in remote areas to the south and west of Veracruz.

One of the supervisors in charge of building the renowned Tehuantepec railroad that would eventually connect the Gulf of Mexico to the Pacific Ocean, McNab was twenty-five years old, with sandy-brown hair and mustache, sparkling blue eyes, a thin aquiline nose, and a cleft in his chin that hinted at a dashing spirit. Eligible bachelors from the railroad company and other foreign enterprises were often invited to gala events by the local elite, and because a *quinceañera* meant the formal introduction of a daughter to society by her family, McNab knew he was sure to meet some beautiful, accomplished young women. In a note to a friend, he wrote: "I received an invitation to a swell ball tonight, so I must brush up my best coat and try to make an impression on some fair señorita."

When María Guadalupe Fuentes Nivon walked into the ballroom, escorted by her father Féderico Nivon, there was unprecedented applause, although she was not the honoree. Nearly five feet seven, she was regal, with thick chestnut brown hair and huge, dark eyes that were framed by beautiful brows. She wore a stylish European silk gown, along with a much-cherished pearl necklace that had belonged to her great-grandmother in France. She was a student at a convent school, spoke three languages, was accomplished at needlepoint, played the piano, and had a wonderful singing voice. John George McNab felt a jolt, that mythic thunderbolt of attraction and respect that was always described in romantic novels; his feelings blazed like the comet that would streak across the sky a few years later.

Dancing and laughing together as the new century began, the

John George McNab was born in Scotland, and came to Mexico to
find fortune and adventure. (Photo source: Family collection.)

couple shared brief stories of their pasts—landscapes that included
mists, moors, alps, and jungles, in Scotland, France, and the Isthmus of
Tehuantepec, and ancestors who had been imaginative and courageous
enough to leave Europe to make their fortunes in the New World. They
agreed to meet again to learn more, but knew that Guadalupe's schooling
and McNab's immediate endeavors might delay their opportunity to
pursue their friendship.

McNab was immersed in Pearson's new railroad project; he was
certain that linking the two oceans that touched Mexico's shores would
have a powerful impact on future trade routes, including the potential
control of Central and South America.

The vision was not new. Several centuries ago, King Charles V suggested to conquistador Hernán Cortés that a means of connecting the two oceans to the east and west of Mexico could be of value. Following royal orders, Cortés explored the Coatzacoalcos River to its source on the Isthmus of Tehuantepec, the narrowest portion of Latin America north of Panama. Along with his soldiers, he took several captives from Tabasco on the journey, including a local princess named Marina, who became his mistress and interpreter. With her help, Cortés learned that the distance across the isthmus was just over one hundred miles. He reported that if a strait could be built, it would be of "immense utility" to his Imperial Majesty. Others realized the potential as well, and in 1774, Spanish Viceroy Antonio M. de Bucareli ordered engineer Agustín Cramer to conduct a survey of the area to see if a canal could be built.

María Guadalupe Fuentes Nivon was one of the most beautiful young women in the state of Oaxaca. (Photo source: Family collection.)

But it wasn't until after Mexican independence that President Santa Anna, recognizing the desirability of interoceanic communication, ordered a careful study of the region in 1833, and authorized a concession to Italian engineer Gaetano Moro in 1842. Throughout the nineteenth century, the canal idea continued to spark interest among Mexicans as well as politicians and entrepreneurs from the United States, and each new president of Mexico commissioned studies and awarded concessions to a variety of companies to pursue the project. While the concessions and studies did not produce any tangible results, the vision survived, and when a US company successfully linked the Pacific and Atlantic oceans in Panama in 1855 with a new railroad, the vision was revised.

Construction of the Tehuantepec Railroad would realize a centuries-old dream to connect the Atlantic and Pacific oceans, establishing an important new trade route. (Photo source: Family collection.)

Growing competition between Great Britain and the United States as the dominant power in the Caribbean and Central America, interest in both intercontinental and international commerce, and issues of national security caused both nations to focus on the strategic isthmus that includes the southeastern parts of the states of Veracruz and Oaxaca, and small parts of Chiapas and Tabasco.

The whole region was hot and malarial, except for the open elevations, where wind from the Pacific Ocean rendered the weather comparatively cool and healthy. The northern side was especially swampy and densely covered with jungle, which posed a major obstacle to the construction of a canal. Eventually both engineers and capitalists realized that the huge cost of a canal was impractical, and the Mexican government looked for another way to establish a transit route through the isthmus.

The newly completed railroad connecting Veracruz to Mexico City was enjoying huge success, and several concessions to build a railroad were granted to various operators over the next few years, but they either failed or were rescinded.

By this time the Mexican government had already spent millions of pesos on the "inter-oceanic route," with disastrous results. Despite US interest in the project, an exasperated President Porfirio Díaz sought a solution through his personal friend Sir Weetman Pearson.

A highly respected civil engineer and contractor, Pearson ran Britain's largest engineering firm, S. Pearson & Son Ltd., based in London. He had succeeded where others had failed, not only in building the monumental drainage canal for Mexico City, but also in the difficult rehabilitation of the port of Veracruz. If anyone could save the Tehuantepec Railway project it was Pearson. Renowned for his business acumen, he negotiated a construction contract with the Mexican government in 1896 that also gave the British engineering firm the right to manage the railway, ports, and dry dock for a period of fifty years. Work commenced in 1899, supervised by Pearson's loyal director in Mexico, John Body, and a young man from Scotland who had been highly recommended to Pearson by his close friend P. W. Thomson.

Thomson was a large landowner in Texas, originally from Scotland, who knew the McNab family well and had hired John George shortly after he graduated from the University of Wisconsin. McNab had wanted to work in a hot, dry climate because of his allergies, and the large and well-respected Thomson Ranch near Eagle Pass suited him perfectly.

Just out of college, he started as a ranch hand, despite his parents' reservations about the rough and tumble world of southwest Texas. Just the year before, newspaper articles in their hometown of Evanston, Illinois, had carried the dramatic story about an outlaw named Dick Duncan who had been hanged in Eagle Pass for the cold-blooded murder of a family from neighboring San Saba. The Texas Rangers had caught him, and the details of his killings were gruesome. The senior McNabs worried about the dangers, and recognized how truly remote the ranch was. A stagecoach line between Eagle Pass and San Antonio had been the only means of transportation until less than a decade ago. Thankfully, in 1882 the main line of the Galveston, Harrisburg & San Antonio Railway was extended to Eagle Pass, with a new connection to the Mexican Railway in Piedras Negras, Mexico. Thomson was excited about the increased international trade; the McNabs were glad their son would not be totally stranded in the "wild west." They shuddered to think that the town had not even had a courthouse until 1885, when a well-known San Antonio architect had been hired to build it for the staggering sum of $20,489. It was there that the infamous Dick Duncan had stood trial.

The *Ferrocarril Veracruz* was Mexico's first railroad,
connecting Mexico City to its most important port, Veracruz.
(Photo source: General Bernardo Reyes, *El General Porfirio
Díaz,* J. Ballesca y Compañía, México, 1903.)

The same year the courthouse was completed, Thomson came up with a project to build a huge gravity-flow irrigation network that would draw water from the Rio Grande River, to convert the brushland of south Texas into fertile farms growing onions, alfalfa, cotton, and even figs. He formed the Eagle Pass Irrigation Company and hired a government engineer to survey the site and estimate the costs of the project. In 1889, Thomson began work; he completed three miles of canal before the project was stalled by lack of funds. Not daunted, the Scottish rancher tried to raise money by forming a company of English investors known as the South-West Texas Water Supply and Land Company Ltd., and he acquired permits from both the United States and Mexican governments. He brought an expert named Robert Wallace all the way from the University of Edinburgh to analyze the soils of Maverick County and the feasibility of the project. Professor Wallace's report was favorable, but Thomson's financial negotiations were thwarted by the outbreak of the Boer War and the economic panic in Europe.

Thomson was delighted to discover that young John George McNab was willing to come to Eagle Pass. His engineering abilities would be valuable if the irrigation project moved forward, and he had indicated a willingness to start as a ranch hand, which pleased his fellow Scotsman.

In 1890, McNab left Illinois bound for Texas. He watched the long, muddy Mississippi River meander outside the window of his railroad compartment, and spent a few days in each major city along the way. New Orleans was sophisticated and glamorous, with quite a nightlife; San Antonio reflected its Mexican influences, with all the modern conveniences, including several attractive restaurants and a new hospital. The final one hundred miles of the journey took him southwest to Eagle Pass, where miles and miles of sage and mesquite stretched as far as he could see. Arriving at sunset, McNab was struck by the hues of mauve, pink, purple, and fading gold that seemed to soften the austere brush country. He straightened his coat and tie, gave his hair a quick brush, and prepared to meet his new employer.

McNab spent six years working on the ranch, and Mr. and Mrs. Thomson treated him like a family member. By 1895 he had been elevated to managing fifty thousand head of sheep and ten thousand head of cattle, handling all the finances of the ranch, and promoting

John George McNab (left) was hired as a ranch hand, but was soon promoted
to manager of the Thomson Ranch. (Photo source: Family collection.)

the innovative "canal project." The journey to San Antonio took only
a few hours on the train, and during days off, there were opportunities
to meet other young men and women at social parties and debutante
balls. And with the little village of Piedras Negras located just across
the Rio Grande and so many Mexicans immigrating to nearby ranches,
McNab soon became fluent in Spanish.

Impressed with his productivity and engineering skills, Thomson
realized that McNab deserved a career with more potential than
working on the ranch could provide. He wrote a letter to his close
friend Weetman Pearson, who happened to be the largest contractor in
the world, recommending that he hire his valued protégé.

In his letter of recommendation, Thomson shared McNab's skills and
previous responsibilities, and added: "My confidence in him was always
implicit. He was always frank, obliging, energetic and conscientious

in whatever capacity he filled. I shall always be grateful to learn of his promotions and advances and I am sure you will never have cause to regret his employment."

With Pearson projects in places like Abyssinia, Arabia, Argentina, Borneo, China, Cyprus, Egypt, India, and Mexico, the company worked in all the key sectors of the economy—oil, railroads, electricity, drainage and irrigation, waterworks and sewers, highways, bridges, and ports. When John George McNab joined S. Pearson & Son Ltd. in 1896, he knew he had found both the opportunity and the adventure he was looking for.

He joined John Body in Veracruz and spent many weeks riding horseback through the isthmus, recruiting laborers for the new railroad project and overseeing equipment and construction. The endeavor was ambitious, involving reconstruction of railroad track that had been laid during earlier failed concessions, as well as the construction of two new modern ports. On the Gulf Coast, Puerto México (today Coatzacoalcos) was a thriving town of twenty-four hundred located on the navigable Coatzacoalcos River, but its new harbor works had to be designed to protect the docks, and vessels anchored there, from the devastating hurricanes that swept through from the Gulf of Mexico.

On the Pacific side, Salina Cruz's harbor faced expensive construction costs, requiring a thirty-three-hundred-foot breakwater to provide four thousand feet of quay space. The town would have to be relocated away from the water's edge, and the new Salina Cruz would receive professional urban planning and a modern water supply and drainage system, all provided by S. Pearson & Son Ltd.

John George McNab moved back and forth across the isthmus, watching the construction of this huge project, convinced that soon the new rail and port service would allow merchandise to be unloaded in one port and loaded onto a ship in the other port within twenty-four hours. But severe hurricanes and an earthquake hit the isthmus in the fall of 1902, partially destroying the newly built station at Salina Cruz and damaging a number of bridges and dredges. Exhausted from the

Weetman Pearson (front row, center) assembled a team of young engineers to build a railroad that would connect Mexico's two oceans; John George McNab (second row, second from left) joined the team in 1896. (Photo source: Family collection.)

winds that gusted at gale force, the constant rain, and long hours spent assessing the setback, McNab longed for the comforts of civilization, and for the company of Guadalupe Nivon, and her beautiful smile.

As the Christmas holidays approached, he received an invitation to Santa Yfigenia, the Nivon family estate in Oaxaca where Guadalupe's widowed grandmother lived. He accepted with alacrity, planning the next step of the courtship he was determined to orchestrate. With gifts in hand, and a very well-brushed coat, John George McNab entered the courtyard of the hacienda, admiring its blooming gardens and impressive façade. He noticed that one symmetrical wing was in disrepair and the splendid fountain was no longer maintained, both clear evidence of a glorious past and a more precarious condition in 1902. Inside were family members to meet, stories to share, mysteries to solve, and a formal procedure for all of it.

Anastacia Fuentes de Nivon, Guadalupe's grandmother, welcomed him in what was once an elegant library. Still furnished with fine

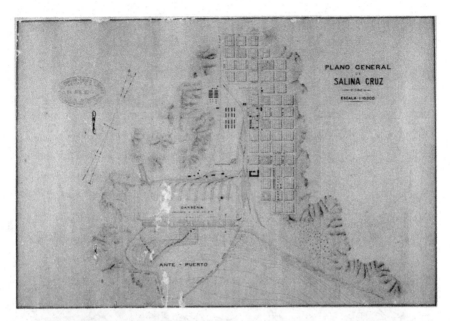

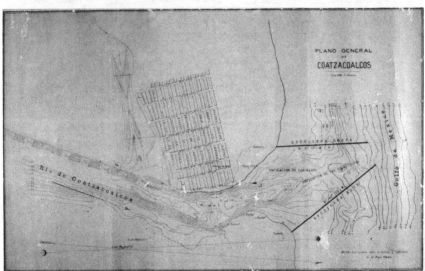

McNab and the Pearson team created new maps for the port cities of Coatzacoalcos and Salina Cruz, which had to be redesigned to accommodate the new Tehuantepec Railroad. (Photo source: Family collection.)

French furniture, a well-polished grand piano, and bookshelves filled with volumes in French, Spanish, and English, it was inviting despite its somewhat worn appearance. Although the great Nivon fortune, built

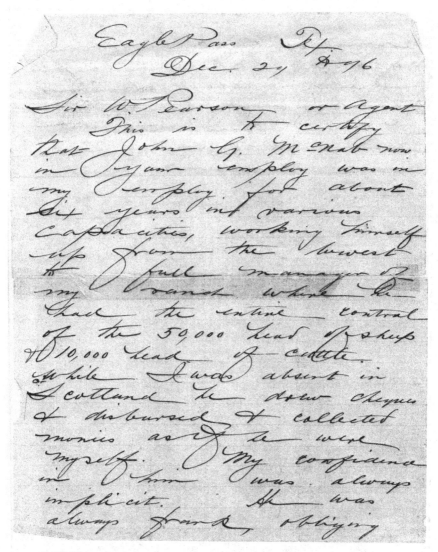

P. W. Thomson, a Scotsman who had employed John George McNab
on his large ranch in south Texas, wrote to Weetman Pearson to
recommend McNab for employment in the British firm's growing
Mexico division, where good engineers were needed for numerous
infrastructure projects. (Photo source: Family collection.)

on the manufacturing of textile dyes and on exports to Europe, had
disappeared by the centennial, a servant passed steaming cups of *chocolate*
as the matriarch introduced McNab to the family members who lived

with her at Santa Yfigenia—her youngest son Luís (Guadalupe's uncle), his wife, and their eighteen-year-old son Carlos. The extended family, including granddaughter Guadalupe, had come from homes all over the isthmus; in all, twenty-three people gathered for a formal dinner.

The Santa Yfigenia hacienda was built by Antoine Nivon for his bride, Anastacia Fuentes, whose deep roots in Oaxaca helped build an immense fortune in the 1800s. (Photograph of historic ruins of Santa Yfigenia: Family collection)

McNab learned that Guadalupe's parents, Federico and Gertrudis Nivon, had produced twelve children but that not all survived childhood due to the very high mortality rate in the humid, disease-ridden region of the isthmus, where malaria, yellow fever, and cholera were rampant. Her father owned a farm near Juchitán, in Oaxaca, and her mother was a native of nearby Tehuantepec. Her grandfather, Antoine Nivon, had immigrated to Mexico from France in 1836, had married the elegant Anastacia Fuentes, and had become an *hacendado,* lord of the great estate called Santa Yfigenia. Guadalupe promised to tell John George the whole story over the next few days. First, however, the Nivon family wanted to know about McNab and his family. Blue eyes twinkling, he began to talk about mists, moors, and castles in Scotland.

"I remember the family story of my great-grandfather's desire to immigrate to America to avoid the compulsion of military service for his sons. It is my understanding that he was so unsettled by his own service in India that he wanted to spare his children this experience."

Judith Virginia Grafius Griffith
Granddaughter of Guadalupe and John George McNab

Chapter 2

Mists and Moors

Scotland: 1800s

The same year that Queen Victoria was crowned in Westminster Abbey, London, John McNab Sr. was born in Perth, Scotland. Both events in 1838 were momentous for the McNab family—Great Britain had a new monarch, and Charles and Ellen Lowe McNab had a first child, a blue-eyed baby son with the famous McNab cleft in his chin, who immediately became the new ruler of their hearts.

The McNab family crest and tartan had a rich history in Scotland, despite the fact that an early dispute with legendary monarch The Bruce cost the family its lands. (Photo source: Family collection.)

McNab worked as a confidential clerk, with an office in the center of Perthshire's largest city and a well-appointed home within walking distance. His study was filled with books and historic maps, and he spent many evening hours reading and imagining faraway places. A contemporary of internationally known Scottish author Sir Walter Scott, McNab had read all of his novels and was especially fond of *Rob Roy*, a tale of daring adventure in the Scottish highlands. A good storyteller himself, he often shared bits of the McNab family history with his children, tracing it as far back as the seventh century, when the name Mac-an-Abba (Son of the Abbot) was first entered into the public record as a landowner, the son of the secular abbot of St. Fillians Parish.

Historic documents about the McNab clan date back to seventh-century Scotland, reflecting colorful ancestry, diverse land holdings, and this ancient burial ground located near Killin, at the base of Loch Tay. (Photo source: Family collection.)

The McNab fortunes changed in the eighth century when, according to legend, a Baron McNab fought against The Bruce and took his brooch, making it the new family emblem of the McNab clan. When The Bruce won the monarchy, the McNabs were stripped of their lands as punishment for their theft of the brooch. By the 1300s they had been forgiven, and records show that a Gilbert McNab received land near Glendochart, as a charter from King David II (Bruce). More land was awarded over the next centuries near Killin, and the McNabs were strongly aligned with the ruling Stuarts. They fought for the royal cause in the civil war, and again felt a downturn of fortune when the other side won. While historic facts were sketchy, these tales of adventure made great bedtime stories that would be passed down for generations to come. They encouraged young John to imagine a future that incorporated some of the romantic elements of heroes like Rob Roy and the famous Red Fox. His sister Isabella, just one year younger, and brother Charles, born in 1840, were ideal for the games he invented. Like most firstborn children, John usually made himself the hero, Isabella the queen or damsel in distress, and Charles the villain who lost every battle.

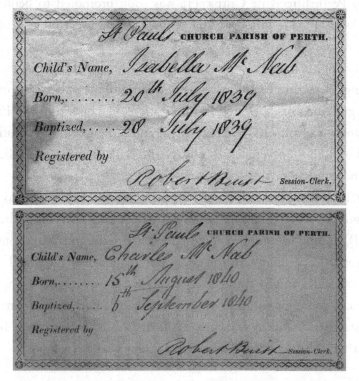

John McNab's two siblings were born in Perthshire—Isabella in 1839, followed by baby Charles in 1840. (Photo source: Family collection.)

Rail service between Glasgow and Edinburgh began in 1842, and the following year, *The Economist* was established by James Wilson, a hatmaker from the small Scottish village of Hawick, who used the new publication to campaign against the new Corn Laws. When John was ten years old, Queen Victoria leased the beautiful Balmoral Estate to the north, which she later bought in 1853 for 31,500 pounds sterling. Scotland's last great outlaw, Ewan MacPhee, died in Fort William when John was twelve, and his dramatic escapades were publicized posthumously in all the newspapers of the day. Even more exciting were the accounts of David Livingstone's discovery of *Mosi-oa-Tunya* ("the water that thunders") in darkest Africa. The Scottish explorer renamed the extraordinary waterfall Victoria Falls, in honor of his queen.

John McNab began to dream of faraway places and adventure, and in 1863, the twenty-five-year-old enrolled as an ensign in the Eighth Perthshire Rifle Corps. He was soon promoted to lieutenant and was assigned to duty in India, a faraway land every bit as exotic as Livingstone's Africa.

Tales of life in India had fascinated the British public since the first drawings depicting elephant fights and sumptuous palaces belonging to Mogul emperors appeared in publications in London in the 1820s. Descriptions of the "Raj" were colorful and quite grand, and could be traced back to the seventeenth century and the formation of the British East India Company.

In 1614 King James had sent his personal envoy, Sir Thomas Poe, to negotiate with Emperor Jahangir (whose son later built the Taj Mahal), hoping to establish trade between Britain and India. But the emperor was not interested, and could not imagine anything the British had that India might want. Poe persisted, however, and eventually convinced Jahangir to allow trade. The British East India Company was established, and by the early 1700s it had its own army in India, consisting of British troops and native soldiers called "sepoys."

The Right Honorable George William Fox, Lord Kinnaird, K.T., &c., &c., &c., Her Majesty's Lieutenant, and High Sheriff of the Shire of Perth.

To *Lieutenant John McNab*

By Virtue of the Power and **Authority** to me **Given, by** Her Most Gracious Majesty Queen Victoria, by Her Commission of Lieutenancy and High Sheriffship of the Shire of Perth, under the Seal appointed to be kept and used in Scotland, in place of the Great Seal thereof, dated the Nineteenth day of March, Eighteen Hundred and Sixty Six, hereby **Appoint** and **Commission** you, the said *John McNab*

to be *Captain* in the *8th Perthshire Rifle Volunteer Corps*

and you, the said *John McNab* having accepted of the said Commission, are carefully and diligently to discharge the duty of *Captain* in the said *8th Perthshire Rifle Volunteer Corps* and are to observe and obey all such orders and directions as, from time to time, you shall receive from your superior Officers, according to Law and the Articles of War.

Given under my hand at *Elcho Hill Lanarkshire twenty seventh* day of *May* in the *Thirty fourth* year of Her Majesty's Reign, and in the year of our Lord, Eighteen Hundred *and seventy one*

Kinnaird

In 1863, John McNab joined the Eighth Perthshire Rifle Corps, was quickly promoted to lieutenant and left for duty in India. He returned to Scotland with honors and was promoted to captain before pursuing a new career in banking. (Photo source: Family collection.)

With factories, forts, and settlements in Bombay, Calcutta, and Madras, the company grew huge, trading in cottons, silks, and indigo, and making inroads into the Dutch domination of the spice market. An "Anglo-Indian" society was developing, and by the end of the eighteenth century, the thriving firm of British merchants was essentially ruling India.

Helen Beattie grew up on a beautiful estate in Cocklarachy, Huntly; her maternal grandmother, Helen Peatt, lived in a castle in Norham-on-Tweed. This portrait was done in 1850, when young Helen was eight years old; it is signed by William Niddrin, but is thought to have been painted by Niddrin's teacher, renowned Scottish portrait painter Sir Henry Raeburn. (Photo source: Family collection.)

Not surprisingly, resentment over Britain's power began to build, and it erupted in 1857 when the British government annexed some additional areas in northern India and issued a new kind of rifle cartridge to its troops and the native sepoy soldiers. When the sepoys learned that the cartridges were greased with pig and cow fat—unacceptable to Hindus and Muslims—they mutinied, massacring as many British as they could find. The uprising spread, and only about eight thousand of the original 140,000 sepoy troops remained loyal to the British. Brutal, bloody atrocities were described in British newspapers, and more troops were dispatched to India to put down the rebellion. By 1858, Delhi was in ruins, but calm had been restored. The East India Company was abolished, and the British crown had assumed the rule of its colony. Historians note that the British government never planned to take control of India, but when British interests were threatened, it had no choice. Queen Victoria appointed a ruling viceroy, and reforms were instituted in an attempt to build conciliation.

Just five years into this uneasy peace, Lieutenant John McNab arrived in Delhi. During his course of duty, he saw British systems of education, finance, and justice introduced, as well as social customs that appealed to the wealthy Indian maharajas who had cast their lots with the British. He wrote home to describe some of the "curiosities" he had read about before his journey and now had seen firsthand—bejeweled emperors, fighting elephants, "charmed" snakes, and all the colors and energies of a place that looked nothing like Scotland.

Harmony, whether real or perceived, was the code of conduct, carefully built into everyday activities, and real trouble between Britain and India would not erupt again for several more decades, when Lord Curzon was appointed viceroy in 1898, mandating the unpopular policies that instigated the national movement that would eventually gain independence for India in 1947. But even in those earlier years of influence, McNab saw exploitation in Britain's rule over a majestic land and did not like being part of the force that made it possible. Still, he served with loyalty for four years and brought back military honors in 1867, earning a promotion to captain.

Helen Elizabeth Beattie was twenty-five years old when she married banker John McNab in 1868. (Photo source: Family collection.)

McNab returned from India disenchanted with military life, and with a new appreciation for the cool mists of Scotland. He was twenty-nine years old, determined to establish a new career and begin his own family. When the Bank of Scotland offered him a position in its Aberdeen branch, he accepted with delight. His intelligence and attention to detail soon earned him a large customer base, including a wealthy gentleman farmer named Alexander Beattie. He was married to Easton Peatt Beattie, whose family owned a successful linen business and a castle near Norham-on-Tweed, not far from Saint Andrews where golf was formalized in 1754.

John McNab and Helen Elizabeth Beattie McNab were a distinguished couple in Crieff, a booming market center in nineteenth-century Scotland, but they dreamed of even greater opportunities for their growing family on the other side of the world. (Photo source: Family collection.)

The McNab family lived in Crieff, a booming financial center in the 1800s. (Photo source: Family collection.)

John George McNab was born at Hawkshaw Cottage in 1871. He grew up
surrounded by tradition, including the green and red tartan plaid that had
represented the family for centuries. (Photo source: Family collection.)

The Beatties' estate was in Cocklarachy, Huntly, with livestock and
cotton in its fields and fragrant heather growing wild. They had ten
children, including an intelligent and serious daughter who was five
years younger than John McNab.

After a whirlwind courtship, Helen Elizabeth Beattie married the
handsome banker in 1868. The groom was tall and carried himself with
an almost-military formality; the bride was so petite that she barely
reached his shoulder. The same year, McNab became manager of the
Bank of Scotland in Crieff, which was regarded as one of the country's
main financial centers.

Situated between the highlands and the lowlands, it was a busy
market town with farmers coming from as far away as Skye to trade
their livestock. The Glenturret Distillery, built in 1775, was a major
employer, and Drummond Castle, with its extraordinary gardens, was
located just to the south of Crieff. The McNabs settled into a roomy and
comfortable home known as the Hawkshaw Cottage, in preparation for

In 1880, John McNab decided to move to the United States with his wife and children. Young John George was nine years old, accustomed to Scottish tradition, but ready for the new adventure. (Photo source: Family collection.)

the large family they hoped to have. In 1869 their first child was born. They named him Charles Alexander in honor of his two grandfathers, but he died shortly after birth, a victim of the high infant mortality rate of the times. On March 22, 1870, Easton Beattie was born, and this first daughter was named in honor of her maternal kin.

John George was born next, on August 27, 1871, followed by a little brother named Joseph Lowe, who was born on Christmas Day of the following year. The next child, William Duncan, died at birth in 1876, and a year later Helen Elizabeth was born on February 16, 1877, followed by the baby of the family, Isabella Lowe, born on March 26, 1878.

As the decade drew to a close, a McNab cousin who had moved to the United States urged John and Helen to join him in "the new world where anything is possible." The death of Helen's father, Alexander Beattie, in 1876, provided his heirs with a substantial inheritance and the opportunity to undertake an adventure like the move to America.

Andrew Carnegie's humble birth in Dunfermline, Scotland, and his extraordinary rise to wealth in the United States fueled the dreams of fellow Scotsman John McNab. (Photo source: Wikimedia Commons; Attribution: user:kilnburn.)

The success of Scotsman Andrew Carnegie in the United States already was legendary; everyone in Scotland was proud of the countryman who was fast becoming one of the richest men in the world. Carnegie was born in Dunfermline in 1835, the son of a handloom weaver who believed strongly in self-education and political activism. Andrew's uncle, George Lauder, a grocer in the same village, shared similar values and taught his nephew Scottish history and introduced him to the writings of Robert Burns.

With the advent of the factory system in the 1840s, weavers were required to work in factories rather than their homes. William Carnegie resisted the change, and when protest efforts failed, he took his family to the United States, settling in Allegheny, Pennsylvania. Both William and his thirteen-year-old son Andrew went to work in a cotton mill, but Andrew's early exposure to books and learning inspired him to find a way to continue his education despite long hours of menial labor. When he discovered that Colonel James Anderson, a wealthy retired military man, offered working boys the opportunity to study in his private library on Saturday nights, Andrew accepted with gratitude. He vowed that someday he would help other working-class citizens achieve an education, and decades later he did just that. He built New York City's first library, and established the Carnegie Foundation to carry out his promise for posterity.

When Carnegie left the mill, he took a number of other jobs, moving from telegraph messenger to telegraph operator with the Pennsylvania Railroad Company, before rising to superintendent of the Pittsburgh Division of the railroad. He invested in railway sleeping cars, and then invested those profits in an oil field in Pennsylvania. By 1868, the year that John and Helen McNab were married, Carnegie had moved heavily into the steel industry, introducing the revolutionary Bessemer steelmaking process into the United States from the United Kingdom, an innovation that had put him on a fast track to more than doubling his fortune.

Stories about other Scotsmen who had made their mark in the new world were even more relevant to the McNab family. Sir Allan Napier McNab served as prime minister of Canada from 1854 until 1856, and later was elected to the Upper House and chosen to be its speaker. His grandfather, Major Robert McNab, had owned property at the head of Loch Earn and was a member of Scotland's famous Black Watch Regiment, eventually serving as his country's "Royal Forester." His father was born at Dundurn, served in Her Majesty's Seventh Regiment, fought in the Revolutionary War, and accompanied General Simcoe to Canada in the late 1700s, establishing a place in the new world for the McNab clan.

About the same time, Archibald, thirteenth Laird of McNab, was born in Bouvain, Glen Dochart. When his illustrious uncle Francis, twelfth Laird of McNab, died without heirs in 1816, Archibald inherited the title along with insurmountable debts. He fled to Canada, where other members of the clan had settled in McNab Township, Renfrew County, Ontario, and where his first cousin, eighteen-year-old Allan, had already fought against the Americans when they invaded Canada in 1812, and was preparing to study law and enter a life in politics. Other branches of the McNab family had immigrated farther south, to the United States.

With five children ranging in age from ten years old to a toddler, John and Helen McNab decided to embark on a great adventure, inspired by the potential that awaited them on the other side of the Atlantic Ocean. Reassured by the presence of cousins who had already settled there, and the knowledge that their sons could avoid the compulsion of military service in America, they left Crieff in 1880, traveling by train to Glasgow.

The family boarded the *Oceanic*, the pioneer vessel introduced by the White Star Line just a few years earlier. It was a three-thousand-ton iron steamship that had created a sensation with its first-class dining saloons and cabins, and quieter engines. The departure from a land that had been home to the McNabs and Beatties for centuries was poignant, and the other passengers onboard also reflected the diverse emotions that a trans-Atlantic voyage to a new life naturally provokes. As the crowd of travelers gathered on the decks, the sound of the ship's great bell rang out. The steward called "All ashore!" and friends and family who were staying behind left the ship with smiles, kisses, handshakes, and some tears. Creeping slowly away from the pier, the steamer started its journey to New York, which could take anywhere from two to five weeks, depending on weather. The parting gun was fired; passengers waved their handkerchiefs to those on shore, and the McNab family watched Scotland disappear in the distance.

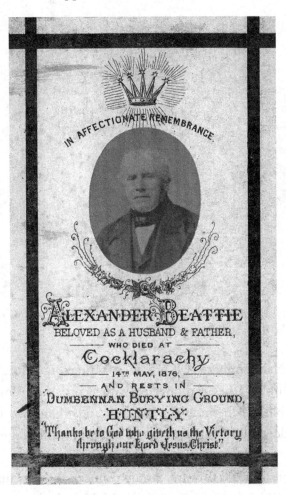

Soon after Alexander Beattie died in 1876, the McNabs decided to invest their inheritance in the New World. (Photo source: Family collection.)

The staterooms of the 1880s were described in advertising brochures as "like the finest Swiss hotel room," and there were parlors, smoking rooms for the gentlemen, and several dining rooms on the vessel. The two oldest McNab children, Easton and John, were allowed to explore the ship together; they were fascinated by the vastness of the sea and their ability to cross it. Both stared in wonder at the huge icebergs off the coast of Greenland, a vision they would remember and describe for the rest of their lives.

The family settled in Evanston, Illinois, and McNab Sr. became secretary of the Rock Island Railway. (Photo source: Family collection.)

The McNab family settled briefly in Minnesota before moving to Evanston, Illinois. They reconnected with Scottish cousins who were already established in the United States, and, thanks to the Beattie estate, dividends and other financial support came regularly from Scotland.

In the late 1800s, as always, family connections were important in terms of finding employment, and the McNabs had some important ones through their Scottish "network." Their move to Evanston enabled

John McNab Sr. to accept the position of secretary of the Rock Island Railway, a direct result of the excellent credentials and connections that he brought to the United States.

All of the McNab children graduated from various universities, and everyone except John George stayed in the Evanston and Chicago areas. They missed their adventuresome brother, in faraway Texas, imagining him living in the "wild west," which was a pretty accurate description of Eagle Pass in the late 1800s. When news reached them that he was going farther south, to Mexico, they realized the opportunity for reunions would diminish, but they were proud that John George would soon be working for the largest engineering company in the world, S. Pearson & Son. The British company already had earned quite a reputation for its international constructions jobs, and its founder had recently been written about in the *New York Times*.

Pearson, the grandson of a British bricklayer, had become well known and wealthy by solving seemingly impossible construction engineering problems. Born in Huddersfield, a small town in northern England, in 1856, he was raised in a middle-class home that encouraged education and remembered the family's humble beginnings despite his father's growing success in the construction business. He excelled in secondary school and was especially gifted in mechanics and math.

When he was sixteen years old, he left school and joined his father's company, S. Pearson and Son, learning the business by observation and hands-on experience, which was often the custom of those times. His father recognized Pearson's remarkable problem-solving skills, and often put him in charge of projects for the company that he would someday own. By 1884, young Pearson had taken charge, and he moved the company to London to compete for new international business. The first of these projects was a dry dock in Halifax, Nova Scotia, built in 1886 for 270,000 pounds, followed by the Avila and Salamanca Railroad in Spain in 1888, for 950,000 pounds, and the Hudson River Tunnel in New York.

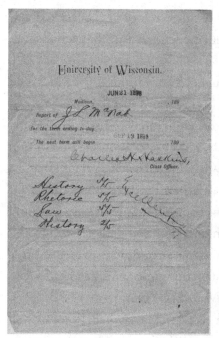

John George excelled in his studies at the University of Wisconsin. He and younger brother Joseph were dashingly handsome, and looking for adventure in 1893. (Photo source: Family collection.)

In 1889, Pearson was temporarily paralyzed after tunneling under the Hudson River to inspect his company's work. His wife convinced him to recuperate in Mexico, sure that the warm climate and exotic landscape would be a welcome change from the cold landscapes of New York and London. While he may have rested a bit on this serendipitous vacation, his entrepreneurial mind was hard at work, fascinated by Mexico's obvious need for infrastructure. In his memoirs, Pearson described meeting with President Porfirio Díaz during his trip, resulting in a contract for his company to undertake the huge *Gran Canal* project, which would provide much-needed drainage and flood protection for Mexico City.

Realizing this was a little different from the other engineering projects that S. Pearson had executed—mainly railroads, dams, and ports—he looked within his company for someone who could manage

Several Mexican presidents had tried to connect the east and west coasts of Mexico; Porfirio Díaz enlisted the aid of Sir Weetman Pearson in 1896. (Photo source: General Bernardo Reyes, *El General Porfirio Díaz*, J. Ballesca y Compañía, México, 1903.)

this massive new endeavor in Mexico. At the top of the list was John Body, who had degrees in both engineering and law. He had worked on the railroad project in Spain and spoke fluent Spanish, which was a necessity for the work ahead in Mexico. In 1890, Pearson promoted Body to the position of director of the company's new Mexico Operations.

Despite some difficulties with the *Gran Canal* project, including delays, which were almost unheard of for S. Pearson & Son, additional large contracts in Mexico followed. In 1895, the company was awarded the Veracruz harbor project, a three-million-pound construction contract that called for the transformation of the city's outdated port into a "new gateway to Europe."

The Veracruz contract was Pearson's opportunity for diversification in Mexico; he began investing in mining, land ownership, electrical utilities, and transportation in and around Veracruz. And even more important, he began to build the relationships with high-ranking members of the Porfirian elite.

In 1896, the company was awarded a contract for 2.5 million pounds to build the Tehuantepec Railway across the narrow isthmus in Mexico's southernmost region. Pearson loved the technical challenges of the project and urged John Body to hire a first-rate team of engineers that could speak Spanish and that could endure the rough terrain of the remote areas involved.

John George McNab signed on with S. Pearson & Son, delighted to put his engineering degree to work on the new railroad, and ready for adventure in a new world. (Photo source: Family collection.)

Not long after the Tehuantepec Railway contract was signed by President Díaz, Pearson received the letter from his old friend, P. W. Thomson, describing the unique abilities of a young engineer named John George McNab. The timing could not have been better. Pearson asked McNab to come immediately to Veracruz and to join a remarkable international company that would provide engineering challenges in a colorful, exciting new land, with a substantial salary and opportunities to share in the company's future profits. McNab accepted with alacrity and with the best wishes of the Thomson family he left the Texas ranch, promising to keep in touch.

When he met John Body in Veracruz he liked him immediately, recognizing an extraordinary mentor. Already friendly with political officials, Body had grown to love the Mexican culture; John George vowed to follow this example.

The next four years were busy for McNab, with much time spent in the hot and swampy regions of the isthmus, where the long-anticipated Tehuantepec railroad finally was under construction. His engineering skills were valuable in the urban planning of the "new" city of Salina Cruz on the Pacific, which would require relocation, a new harbor, and a modern water and drainage system. The challenges had been many, but one reward had been McNab's introduction to a beautiful *señorita* named Guadalupe Nivon.

When John George told his new friends about the land of his childhood he explained that while he would always cherish the memories of the wild and beautiful country where he was born, he had left the mists and moors of Scotland behind, choosing Mexico for his future and now calling himself Juan Jorge McNab to prove it. Guadalupe's grandmother and aunt asked polite questions about his parents in faraway Evanston, Illinois, and all the Nivons promised to share their family history the next day. As a dramatic finale to the evening, Guadalupe sat down at the antique piano, first playing *"Auld Lang Syne"* in honor of the tale they'd just heard, followed by *"La Marseillaise,"* in honor of the story to come.

"It was market day. She wore a tall white headdress and a full skirt, embroidered with purple and yellow flowers, large hoop earrings of gold, and an ornate necklace. Part of the renowned Fuentes family, whose Rancho Espinal produced the finest vanilla and maize in Oaxaca, Anastacia was an entreprenuer by the time she was fifteen years old."

Antoine Nivon's diary, 1838

Chapter 3

Castles and Kings

France: 1800s

East of France's Rhone Valley, rolling hills, fragrant apricot and cherry orchards, silkworm farms, and unique square farmhouses made from large rounded glacial pebbles have flanked the Drôme River, and the smaller Galaure River, for centuries.

Madame de Sévigné, the great court socialite and correspondent during Louis XIV's reign, spent three long periods of her life in the area, at Chateau de Grignan, located on a hill above the village houses and their surrounding fields of lavender. Her daughter, Françoise-Marguerite, was considered one of the brightest beauties in all of France, inspiring eighteenth-century author La Fontaine to dedicate a fable to her, "*The Lion in Love.*" She married François Comte de Grignan, who spent most of his time at court, spending lavishly, and their daughter was forced to sell the family castle in 1732 to pay off her father's massive debts.

The Nivon family in France could be traced in written record to the year 665; for more than one thousand years, Guadalupe's paternal line had farmed land in La Drôme, not far from Chateau de Grignan, supplying truffles, olives, goat cheese, and fruits to the count and countess, as well as to the local village markets. By the eighteenth century, the Nivons were known for their textiles, especially the silk that was harvested from orchards of mulberry trees each spring.

On January 14, 1811, Jean Antoine Nivon was born in the village of Peyrus, the son of a textile producer and weaver. He and his twin sister, Thérèsè, were the youngest of ten children, and from an early age he understood the importance of land as a source of food and enterprise. A traditional evening meal in the Nivon home consisted of soup made flavorful with pork fat, bread, a half-glass of wine, followed by a small amount of beef with a platter of home-grown vegetables. On special occasions, *gaufes*, dry waffles that are typical of the region, were a treat for the children.

Château de Grignan dominated the landscape of the La Drôme region of France, overlooking fields of lavender and the mulberry trees where the Nivon family raised their silkworms. (Photo source: Wikimedia Commons/Public Domain.)

Napoleon Bonaparte resided at nearby Valence for many months during an early stage of his military career, and he was fond of this area of France. He admired its hardworking people and enjoyed the fruits of their labor, which appeared on sumptuous platters at his table as he entertained in the style of the emperor that he would someday become.

By the time little Jean Antoine Nivon was born, Napoleon's power stretched across Europe and the entire Spanish empire, which included Mexico. This faraway land across the ocean, with its exotic and mysterious possibilities, would someday lure young Nivon away from La Drôme and the landscape his family had occupied for centuries.

In the early years of the nineteenth century, information was scarce outside the big cities. The only news of the world beyond village life came from the merchants who brought their wares from Paris to local markets, or from the entourages of the wealthy families traveling to their summer chateaux. In 1815, a pigeon brought the news of Napoleon's defeat at Waterloo.

But modernization was under way, and just four years later, France adopted freedom of the press and printed news began to flourish. In 1829, Louis Daguerre began to experiment with new photographic methods; *The Poetical Works of Coleridge, Shelley and Keats* was published in Paris, and Louis Braille invented embossed printing for the blind. Information was becoming more available all across Europe, and even small villages began to print local newspapers.

In the late 1820s, printed notices about extraordinary opportunities in the "new world" began to appear in the villages of La Drôme and Haute Saone, regions of France that were well known for their industrious people with skills in farming and textiles. Paid representatives of Compagnie Franco-Mexicaine traveled through the regions to talk about Mexico in particular, and the need for manpower to plant the verdant fields near the Gulf of Mexico.

Advertisements proclaimed that, "nine and one-half months of work in Jicaltepec in 1833 resulted in the planting of 2500 feet of sugar cane and many thousand acres of coffee, with the skills of two intelligent chief cultivators and 6-8 assistants, we predict making at least 60,000 francs this year." Promises of free market exports to foreign countries, duty-free entry for equipment and machines for processing sugar cane, rice, coffee, and other goods, and a flourishing free enterprise system were incentives, along with the reassurance that there was already a church, hospital, and school in the growing French colony.

The dream presented in the bulletin was not a total reality, but shiploads of hopeful dreamers sailed from Le Havre to Veracruz to find out for themselves. The next few years in France were difficult ones. In 1831 a cholera epidemic devastated Paris, and a very cold winter in 1832 caused crop failures. Reports of opportunities in the new world were sounding better and better.

With the expulsion of the Spanish from Mexico in 1828, the French moved quickly to fill the niche in the luxury goods market that was created when the Spaniards departed. That year French exports to Mexico totaled only 7.8 million francs; two years later the figure had more than doubled.

> *Our settlements are located near the Gulf of Mexico, on the Nautla River, just 22 kilometers north of Veracruz. Its fertile valleys are some of the richest in Mexico; and the climate is marvelous. Principal products are:*
>
> o   *Vanilla….an indigenous plant that is easily cultivated*
> o   *Tobacco….without a doubt an industry for grand commerce, of a quality that equals tobacco from Havana*
> o   *Sugar cane…top quality, perfect for rum for export*
> o   *Coffee….cultivated easily throughout the valley*
> o   *Rice, Corn, and More…*

Printed bulletins advertised Mexico's glorious potential in 1833.
(Photo source: Rendering from original bulletin in French.)

Two French consulates were established in Mexico to accommodate the more than four thousand new citizens who had immigrated, located in Xalapa and Veracruz. A consulate general was dispatched to Mexico City, and the three locations reported that 678 French heads of families (not counting their family members) had registered by December 1831.

In 1836, twenty-five-year-old Jean Antoine Nivon decided to join the growing number of his adventuresome countrymen who were immigrating to the new world. He knew that it would be many years before he would see his family or the rolling hills of La Drôme again; he was leaving the old life behind, and it was not easy. But his destination pulled him like a magnet. *México*—the word seemed exotic, a faraway place that would become his home, where new beginnings were certain, and where the future belonged to him.

The journey was hard, with storms and seasickness during the crossing. A letter from a fellow passenger who sailed on the *Sylphide* from Le Havre to Veracruz described arriving in Mexico in 1836:

> "We have arrived and we are very happy, grateful for the attention of our doctor and for the beautiful weather. We have rapidly forgotten our tiredness from the ship and are working with energy towards Christmas and the new year. The land is fertile, and the colonists who arrived before we did have confirmed that the land is good. We see clearly the need to receive help from more colonists and we are writing our families and friends in France, urging them to join us. We are testing growing bananas and sugar cane. We have a vegetable garden, and in the middle of it, we have installed a pump for irrigation."

Other arrivals were not so pleasant, as reported by another adventurer, who traveled from France later in the year:

> "Although the crossing was good, we encountered difficult challenges upon arriving. We did not have immigration permits and were not allowed to disembark at Nuatla. We were sent to Tuxpan, where we were also refused, then to Vera Cruz. Finally after much pleading and perseverance, the officials understood there were a number of infants between six and nine months old on board, and we were allowed to put our feet on our new land."

Many of the new immigrants were demobilized soldiers or dismissed officeholders who had been marginalized when France's borders shrank as the huge Napoleonic bureaucracy and army disbanded. Others were the sons of republican leaders of the French Revolution, who realized they might fare better away from the Crown. The predominant employment was that of artisan or small trader.

According to Mexican law, foreigners could not possess land without giving up their nationality and the protection of their legation, so only colonists willing to do that could become ranchers or farmers. When Antoine Nivon arrived in Veracruz in 1836, he dreamed of being a landowner from the moment his ship docked in the port known as *La Villa Rica de la Vera Cruz*—"the rich city of the true cross"—the gateway to Mexico.

The city's walls were tinted red, yellow, blue, and green, and domes and turrets could be seen from the ship's deck, gleaming like polished marble in the sunshine. Because the day was clear, he could see the volcano of Orizaba nearly sixty miles inland, with its crystal peak at an altitude of 17,500 feet.

Veracruz, with its colorful walls, seemed a magical city to the emigrants arriving in the early 1880s. (Illustration source: F. A. Ober, *Travels in Mexico,* Estes and Lauriat, Boston, MA, 1884)

One of the hottest cities in the country, Veracruz's white streets were kept meticulously clean with a gutter system, and extra care was taken to dispose of garbage, in the hopes that the dreaded presence of *el vómito*—yellow fever—could be avoided. It was reported that people were dying at the rate of one hundred a week, and the port had become known as *la ciudad de los muertos*—"the city of the dead." Vultures, seen by the hundreds, perched on every rooftop. Courage was needed to live in Veracruz, and in addition to the health risks, anyone lucky enough to achieve merchant status faced an outrageous customs duty ordered by the Mexican government. Despite the challenges, young Nivon was determined to be both a landowner and a merchant in this new land.

RUINS OF PAPANTLA.

Nivon explored his new homeland and traveled to ancient cities like Papantla, determined to embrace both his new language and culture. (Illustration source: F. A. Ober, *Travels in Mexico,* Estes and Lauriat, Boston, MA, 1884)

Almost immediately, he found work as a vanilla trader, utilizing the skills he had learned from his family's agricultural business in France. The vanilla plant flourished in the forests on the eastern slopes of the hills beyond Veracruz and was carefully gathered by the locals, who had cultivated it for centuries and supplied it to Montezuma and the Aztec nobility. The ancient culture of these indigenous people produced the nearby pyramid of Papantla, an architectural wonder with a perfect square for a base and a great staircase of fifty-seven steps, as well as the Toltec calendar of 366 days. Famous for architecture, agriculture, and beautiful women, the regions along the Tehuantepec River area shipped their aromatic vanilla to Veracruz, where traders like young Nivon expedited its export. Travel writers of the times described both the scenery and indigenous people in glowing terms. Soon Nivon would prove an old Mexican saying correct: *Las doncellas son muy halagüeñas—* "the women are very bewitching."

But before he found romance in a remote village of the isthmus, inland from Veracruz, he concentrated on his work, learning a new language, and opening his mind to new ideas and cultures. Living in the center of town, Nivon mingled freely with the port city's local citizens, sampling foods that seemed exotic to his palate, and learning Spanish.

Most of his fellow colonists lived in a close-knit enclave in Jicaltepec, just a few kilometers away, where they had established a home life similar to the one they had left behind in La Drôme. Every family made its own bread at least once a week, and Antoine savored the delicious *brioches* and *galettes* that were often left at his door by friends. Whenever he felt homesick, he would wangle an invitation to dinner in the home of a married friend, knowing that the familiar tastes of tripe, in a saltwater marinade; *la potée*, a rich stew of pork, cabbage, beans, potatoes, carrots, peas, and now, in Mexico, the addition of bananas; and a delicious bread pudding with cinnamon, sugar, and cream for dessert would remind him of meals around his family's table, sitting next to his twin sister Thérésè.

At the village level, for the most part life focused on work and the daily occurrences that bond communities together. But on a national level, longstanding bonds were disintegrating. The loss of Texas, which won its independence in 1836, and France's refusal to recognize Mexico's independence created political instabilities, and relations between the French immigrants and Mexican citizens and government grew increasingly strained.

A cholera epidemic several years before was still blamed on the French immigrants, since Paris had suffered an earlier epidemic. In Atencingo, a small village in the state of Puebla, panic-stricken peasants assassinated five French colonists in the mistaken belief that they had poisoned the water supply. The press and public rhetoric urged Mexico to resist being "colonized" by the French, citing the examples of the Berbers and the Algerians, the populations of North Africa over which France had gained control. Mexicans resented France for choosing to honor the Bourbon Family Compact between the French and Spanish monarchs rather than "siding with justice."

The French were outraged at the xenophobia and mistreatment they suffered at the hands of the Mexicans. From Paris, Foreign Minister Mole denounced the situation in a letter to the French consulate general in Mexico City, dated November 7, 1836:

> "It is an example unprecedented in the history of international relations for a country wherein everyone and everything—people, government, courts—yielding to the most base prejudices, seeks to outdo itself in displays of hatred and hostility against foreigners and appears to go out of its way to insult ... the governments from which they come. Such nevertheless is the example of Mexico."

Complaining that Europeans were hounded, ransomed, pillaged, and assassinated "like Jews in the Middle Ages," even though they set an example of civilized industry "in the midst of an ignorant and barbaric society," the French colonists were vocal in their anger. By the time Antoine Nivon arrived in Mexico, relations had deteriorated almost to the point of war.

When the French navy blockaded the harbor of Mexico's main

port of Veracruz in early 1838, the fiscal damage outweighed the physical. The revenues from the customhouses in Veracruz constituted the single largest source of income for the chronically bankrupt federal government. Angered by the French offensive, many Mexicans attacked foreigners in the streets and damaged foreign property, causing many French citizens to return to France or flee to the United States.

Antoine Nivon was not among them. By this time he had fallen in love with a young native woman named Anastacia Fuentes, whose family had a large ranch east of Juchitán, in the heart of the agricultural region of Oaxaca that produced a variety of crops for trade and export. The Fuentes family was legendary for growing the finest vanilla and maize on its Rancho Espinal; and when they traveled to Veracruz to sell their harvests, they organized an elaborate caravan of wagons that carried their children, their finest traditional clothing and gold jewelry for the parties they would attend, and the valuable crops that would be exported from the bustling port to Europe. The journey took more than a week; the caravan stopped in small mountain villages, where cousins welcomed the traders, sometimes joining the long overland trip to the coast.

Anastacia was an exotic beauty, already skilled at commerce, a tradition among the women of Oaxaca. During a visit to Veracruz in 1838, accompanied by her parents and her siblings, she attended a ball honoring a cousin. Several of the foreign-born traders, including Antoine Nivon, were also invited, and when the young Frenchman saw Anastacia moving gracefully on the dance stage with her father, he was struck by her native beauty and graceful movements.

The traditional music of Veracruz was gay, with a pronounced beat, and songs from Spain and from the interior of Mexico were played as well. Following the custom, friends of the honoree approached her and placed a large hat on her head. When permitted this gallantry, the young man earned a dance with the honoree. During the excitement of this activity, Antoine quietly offered his hat to Anastacia. She smiled, and as the band played "*La Buquito*," they shared a first dance, never dreaming

Women from the Isthmus of Oaxaca were known both for their
beauty and business acumen. (Photo source: Family collection.)

that history would repeat itself several generations later when their
granddaughter would meet a handsome foreigner at another *quinceañera*
ball in Veracruz.

The following year, in 1839, they married and settled not far from
Tapanatepec, in the southernmost part of Oaxaca, where Don Antonio
was welcomed wholeheartedly. From the hills above the town, the
view of verdant fields of sugarcane and corn, dotted with white stone
haciendas and Indian hamlets, was beautiful, and the rich soil and
tropical weather made the area an agricultural paradise. In addition to
the cane and corn he saw below, cotton, alfalfa, *arnatto*, sweet potatoes,
cacao, wheat, vanilla, pecans, oranges, and coffee grew well here, and
the Zapotecs had been tilling these crops for centuries.

When Anastacia married Antoine Nivon, she connected him to
the Zapotec "network," which was huge in Oaxaca, and was critical
to the success of any enterprise in the lower half of the state. Members

of her family owned lands near Tehuantepec, Juchitán, Niltepec, and Zanatepec, and the Fuentes name carried with it a respect that ensured the loyalty of the workers that were so essential to the success of a *hacendado*.

Traders traveled from Oaxaca to Veracruz to sell their crops in the port city; the Fuentes family was one of the most successful and entrepreneurial. (Photo source: Family collection.)

Because of his marriage to a Mexican citizen, Nivon was no longer required to pay the heavy taxes or subjected to loans that were forced on foreigners by the government, and he was allowed to own land. He had cast his lot with Mexico, and as Don Antonio Nivon, he acquired the Santa Yfigenia hacienda and moved from the vanilla trade to agriculture and exporting, developing extraordinary natural dyes and textiles that he sold to France and other parts of Europe.

He applied the talents and traditions he brought from France to a new industry that focused on something completely indigenous to his new homeland. Natural dyes, produced from the wealth of plants, and even from insects, which thrived in the lush climate of the isthmus, were a product he understood well from his family's silk enterprise in La Drôme.

The landscape of southern Oaxaca was breathtaking, like nothing Antoine Nivon had seen in France. He had cast his lot with Mexico, becoming Don Antonio, the proud *hacendado* of Santa Yfigenia. (Photo source: Family collection.)

The cochineal insect, which lives in *nopales* or prickly pears, was treasured in the new world for thousands of years. By the fourteenth century the Incas and the Aztecs had developed entire agricultural systems based on cochineal, and they valued the red dye that came from the insects as much as gold. In Europe, the best red colorings were made from another insect, the kermes, which lives in oak trees, but its red color was dull compared to cochineal.

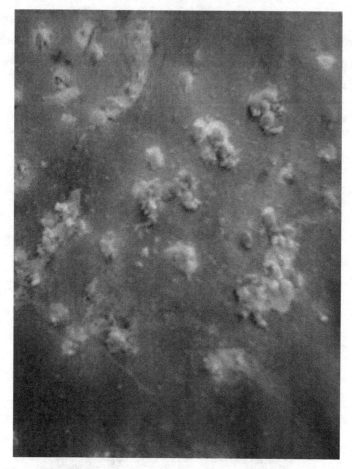

The cochineal insect lives on the *nopal* cactus, and the vivid red dye
it produces was more valuable than gold or silver in the 1400s.

By 1600 cochineal was second only to silver as the most valuable
import from Mexico, and in 1630, it was discovered that treating the
dye with an acidic tin solution made it bond well to fabric. It became
the dye of choice, used to create the scarlet textiles that became elaborate
cardinals' robes in Rome, and used in the British redcoat uniforms of
the American Revolution.

In the mid-1800s, access to cochineal farms was tightly controlled,
but Don Antonio Nivon had the knowledge and skill to be awarded
participation in this booming enterprise. Since his family in La Drôme

had raised silkworms and produced textiles, he was well qualified to build a profitable cochineal operation on the hacienda.

He expanded his dye production to include other natural dyes: a beautiful blue from the indigo plant (*anil*) became immensely popular in Europe, and thousands of hectares of anil were planted at Santa Yfigenia. Huge dye vats were carved in the hollow of the earth at the estate, and the labor-intensive process of making the valuable dye went on year-round. Twice a year, Nivon's caravan of precious dyes made the difficult journey from the lush isthmus to Veracruz, where heavily laden merchant ships transported them to Europe, where they became an important part of the luxury goods market.

President Antonio López de Santa Anna was overthrown in 1855, just two years after he sold seventy-seven thousand square kilometers of Mexico to the United States, keeping most of the money for himself. (Photo source: Library of Congress Prints and Photographs Division, Washington, DC—LC-USZ62-131344.)

Antonio and Anastacia had eleven children who survived childhood, a miracle in the disease-ridden region where one-third of the French sailors who blockaded Veracruz in 1838 became ill with malaria or yellow fever during the summer months. Their fifth child was a son named Federico, born in 1848, just two years after Mexico lost half of its territories to the United States as a result of the war between the two nations.

Like all of the Nivon children, Federico grew up fluent in Spanish, French, and Zapotec, and he loved exploring the grounds of the hacienda and playing inside with his three older sisters and older brother, Antonio. Life at Santa Yfigenia was idyllic, but beyond its high walls, the country was in turmoil.

Following Emperor Agustín's abdication in 1823, Mexico had become a republic, and, after a decade of unrest and near anarchy, Santa Anna was elected president in 1833. Under his leadership, Mexico lost Texas to independence in 1836, and just a little more than a decade later, lost half of its territories during the war with the United States in 1848. In 1853, when Federico Nivon was five years old, President Santa Anna sold seventy-seven square kilometers of Mexico to the United States for $10 million, keeping most of the money for himself. He was overthrown as president just two years later.

Turbulence had become the standard, and between 1822 and 1860 the republic changed presidents more than fifty times and experienced 140 military coups. But Santa Yfigenia and the Nivon family enjoyed relative stability, secure in their production of goods that continued to be very valuable to Mexico's foreign markets.

Following the civil war of 1860, Benito Juárez seized power with the backing of the United States. Mexico suspended repayment of all foreign debt except to the United States, and its principal creditors—France, Britain, and Spain—sent a joint military force to occupy Veracruz in 1861. Juarez gave in, repaid most of the debt, and Britain and Spain withdrew. However France continued the war; troops marched into Mexico City and occupied the country's capital.

The Nivon family remained in an enviable position, with its combined French and indigenous heritage, large land holdings, and a prosperous textile dye export business. Each summer the family sailed to France to escape the worst malaria months in the isthmus, and although Don Antonio's parents had died just three years after he immigrated to Mexico, there were still many aunts, uncles, and cousins in La Drôme who shared all the experiences of the French lifestyle with their Mexican relatives.

As everyone enjoyed a lovely summer picnic on the banks of the Galaure River, Don Antonio remembered his departure from La Drôme nearly thirty years ago, his last glance at Château Grignan, the castle that had dominated the landscape for centuries, and his profound relief that he was leaving Napoleon's empire behind. Little did he know that upon his return to his beautiful Santa Yfigenia at summer's end, French politics would again influence his world, bringing changes that would impact the Nivon fortune for generations to come.

"My mother was especially close to her older sister Gertrudis—my aunt 'Tula'—and her younger sister Guadalupe, who was the most beautiful of the Nivon girls. I have many childhood memories of times spent in the McNab's home in Salina Cruz and at the Nivon Ranch—'Santa Gertrudis' where Aunt Tula lived—just up the coast. Aunt Tula lived to be quite old and she had beautiful teeth; she dipped her finger in salt to brush them."

Millicent Antelma Gertrudis Craigie Keck
Niece of Guadalupe Fuentes Nivon McNab

Chapter 4

Déjà Vu

Mexico: 1860–1900

The Nivon family trip to France in the summer of 1861 was a special one. Don Antonio had celebrated his fiftieth birthday in January; most of his adult life had been spent creating a successful life in a new world, and as he watched his children interact with their French cousins, he felt deep contentment about the choices he had made. Rosalia and Delfina, oldest daughters of the family, had not made the journey this year because they had married and were beginning families of their own. The other eight ranged in age from sixteen to two years old, and from Doña Anastacia's special glow, Don Antonio was nearly certain that another baby would join the family next year.

At thirteen, young Federico was especially intrigued by the customs of La Drôme, showing genuine interest in the farming techniques of the beautiful valley, where silkworms still were an important part of agricultural life. He told his younger cousins about another insect from Oaxaca that was even more amazing, producing *grana cochinilla*, the vivid red dye that the Nivon family shipped to Europe.

The production of indigo dye was equally as lucrative, and Don Antonio's oldest son, Antonio, already helped with the enterprise. He delighted in sharing its complexity with their French cousins, boasting that anil being grown on the hacienda found its way from one of the most remote parts of Mexico to Paris, eventually becoming the famous blue fabrics used to create the most elaborate French fashions.

Antonio and Federico explained that because massive numbers of indigo plants were required to produce fairly small quantities of the deep blue dye, the four-hundred-thousand-acre Santa Yfigenia was well suited for this booming industry. The plant's special requirements for humidity and rainfall were also met perfectly in the wet isthmus region.

Each September, when the leaves were robust, the hacienda's workers carefully pulled them from the plants, guarding them from flies, which with a single touch could ruin them for dye-making. Tall stacks were gathered and left in the sun for a few hours. By the end of a day, more than twenty-five hundred workers had each produced a large mountain of leaves, and they carefully transported them to the giant earthen vats that surrounded the hacienda. Adding cold water, the workers stayed busy for the next two months, stirring the mixture of water and leaves at least ten times a day. The result was a thick paste, which could either be used in the vats to dye fabrics, or could undergo a longer process to produce dye for export.

When the Nivons dyed beautiful fabrics on the hacienda, workers placed silks from Europe or pure cottons from local producers in the vats, adding *ceniza* and *nopal* plants to the paste to set the color. There was always a sense of wonder when watching the process. First the submerged cloth turned a vivid yellow color in the liquid; when it was removed and met the air, it became green. Five minutes later, with cheers from the workers, the brilliant blue textiles made their dramatic appearance.

For dye export, the paste mixture was removed from the vats, shaped into grapefruit-sized balls by hand, and dried in the sun for ten days. Next it was grated into powder, which was packaged for the long journey to the port of Veracruz, where it was shipped to luxury houses across the Atlantic whose customers waited for the very special blue that had taken so many workers so many months to produce.

As summer ended, the Nivons knew the anil leaves were approaching harvesttime at home. They enjoyed the summers abroad, spent in cooler air, surrounded by fields of lavender and apricot trees; but homecoming at Santa Yfigenia was always a time of celebration and deep commitment

Natural dyes, made from plants and even insects, were
the source of the Nivon family fortune.

to their life in the New World. As the autumn of 1861 approached, they
bade their French relatives farewell and started their sea voyage home,
watching the landscape of La Drôme disappear, imagining the fragrant
gardens of the hacienda waiting for them on the other side of their ocean
crossing. They treasured their special Mexican-French heritage, and they
were not the only ones thinking about the bonds between those two
countries in 1861.

Napoleon III was heavily influenced by his romantically minded
Spanish wife, the Empress Eugenie, who was determined to see a
European monarchy revived in Mexico. He liked the idea of placing

someone on the throne that would promote the interests of France and follow his instructions from the other side of the globe. The idea was not new, but there was now real potential for it since the United States was embroiled in a civil war. Prior to 1861, any interference with Mexico by European powers would have been viewed as a challenge to the United States, and no one wanted to risk that. Now the North American power had its own troubles and could not intervene.

Envisioning France as "the civilizing influence" in the Western Hemisphere, and well aware of the financial opportunities, Napoleon III carefully studied the current situation in Mexico. His half brother, the Duc de Morny, was the largest single holder of Mexican bonds, which were worthless as long as Benito Juárez was president, and other ventures confirmed that the Juárez presidency was highly unfavorable to European interests. The Mexican treasury was practically bankrupt, and the country's protector to the north was paralyzed for the moment. Mexico was a vulnerable target.

Empress Eugenie suggested a favorite candidate for the Mexican throne—Archduke Ferdinand Maximilian, the brother of Austrian Emperor Franz Josef, a part of her royal Habsburg lineage. Tall, elegant, and imaginative, Maximilian was born at Schonbrunn Palace in 1832, the second son of Archduke Franz Karl. As a boy he was lively and curious, and he loved the sea. He joined the imperial navy and became its commander in chief, and during his oceanic adventures, he fell in love with a beautiful Brazilian princess named María Amalia. They became engaged to be married, but before the wedding date, she died at the age of twenty-one, leaving the archduke heartbroken.

Three years later, in 1856, he met and married Princess Charlotte of Belgium and built her a beautiful castle, which he named Miramar, just outside Trieste. Surrounded by spectacular gardens, with a magnificent view of the sea, it was both a tribute to his lost love and a symbol of hope for his new marriage. But that hope faded after a journey to Brazil in 1859, when he brought back a venereal disease that would preclude his wife from ever having children. When Napoleon III offered him the crown of Mexico, he understood Charlotte's vehement desire to become an empress, with a built-in escape to a land far away from the unhappiness that had begun to dominate her life in Austria.

Maximilian was uncertain, but Charlotte's determination convinced him; he accepted on the condition that the people of Mexico must want him as their ruler. His brother, Franz Josef, cautioned him, believing it to be a dangerous assignment, and suggested that if Maximilian accepted the offer he should get support in writing from Napoleon III.

In 1864, Archduke Maximilian accepted the imperial crown in Europe; he and his wife, Princess Charlotte would become the new emperor and empress of Mexico. (Photo source: Wikimedia Commons/Public Domain.)

The United States also protested, citing the Monroe Doctrine, but the Civil War prevented any action, just as Napoleon III had predicted. After a "favorable plebiscite" in Mexico, totally orchestrated by the

French, Maximilian accepted the imperial crown at Miramar Castle in 1864.

The new emperor and empress of Mexico set sail on the *M.S. Novara*; and the send-off was spectacular. The Mexican flag flew from the ship's mast, the pope blessed the voyage, and Queen Victoria ordered the garrison at Gibraltar to fire a salute when the ship passed by. In Veracruz they were greeted with wild enthusiasm, and their coronation at *Catedrál Metropolitana* was everything Princess Charlotte—now the Empress Carlota—had dreamed of. Located in the Zócalo (Constitution Square) in Mexico City, the cathedral was on the same site as the Catholic church built by Hernán Cortés, and had been consecrated in 1667. Its new bell towers and central dome, designed by the Spanish neoclassicist architect Manuel Tolsa, were completed in 1813.

Don Antonio and Anastacia Fuentes were among the elegant guests invited to the coronation and the celebrations that followed. The ladies wore extraordinary ball gowns of the finest silk, accessorized with shoes and jewels from France, and the men wore the latest European formal attire.

Dining on gourmet French delicacies and dancing to the waltzes of Johann Strauss, guests talked about their travels abroad, their children's schooling in Europe, and their hopes that the French intervention would bring much-needed financial stability to Mexico's fragile treasury. There were whispers that President Juárez was biding his time in the north, just waiting for help from the United States once its bloody civil war ended.

Many of the country's business leaders and *hacendados* experienced an ambivalence with the new imperial regime, finding ways to coexist with the empire's administration system while remaining loyal to local political structures in their states. Both deposed President Benito Juárez and General Porfirio Díaz were born in Oaxaca; Anastacia's family had connections to them both. And Don Antonio, known for his political savvy and cleverness, was masterful at protecting Santa Yfigenia and the Nivon family's fortune. They made loans to the nationalists and collaborated surreptitiously with the French regime, hoping to come out ahead whichever side ultimately won control of Mexico.

Now officially ensconced in their palace at Chapultepec, the new rulers were enchanted by their new country, proving it by assuming Spanish variations of their names and attempting to adopt two young heirs of the original Mexican imperial dynasty of Emperor Agustín de Iturbide. Hopeful that the Mexican princes would someday succeed them, Maximiliano and Carlota envisioned a Habsburg-Iturbide line that would continue for many generations to come.

Similarly, Don Antonio had embraced Mexico nearly thirty years ago, and all of the Nivon children had been baptized with Spanish names. They considered themselves to be Mexican to the core, equally proud of their mother's indigenous origins on the isthmus and of their father's French forebears. Now major participants in the production of *grana cochinilla* and anil, the most lucrative enterprises in Oaxaca, the Nivons had experienced huge profits, and more than twenty-five hundred peons worked in the fields of Santa Yfigenia by the mid-1800s. More valuable than silver or gold to the Mexican economy, at their zenith the natural dyes sold for five pesos per pound, with a production cost of thirty-two centavos per pound.

With the government's passage of the famous Lerdo laws in 1856, land that had formerly belonged to the Catholic Church was redistributed; historic records indicate that the Nivon and Fuentes families were the recipients of several large parcels in Oaxaca.

Between 1857 and 1863, Antonio and Julio Nivon, sons of Don Antonio y Doña Anastacia, were awarded more than twenty-three thousand acres near Zanatepec, becoming important ranchers in their own right. The lower half of the state was dotted with the villages of Tehuantepec, Juchitán, Niltapec, Zanatepec, and finally Tapanatepec, and there were members of the Fuentes and Nivon families living in them all.

According to legal records of the same period, Don Antonio and "las señoras Fuentes" were involved in a dispute over lands that had once belonged to the Dominican order of Nuestra Señora del Rosario near Tenesten. Several other *hacendados* also claimed ownership, but ultimately the judge ruled in favor of the Nivons when Don Antonio's agent, Alejandro de Gyves, presented ownership documents for Santa Yfigenia and another ranch known as La Lagunilla.

On the Isthmus of Oaxaca, especially in the Juchitán District, the native culture was known for its strong women. The women actively acquired lands, and they were famous for their independence and business abilities. They controlled local commerce and demonstrated their prosperity by wearing elaborate gold jewelry and the intricate traditional dresses from the region that artist Frida Kahlo would someday make world famous. Anastacia Fuentes was one of these remarkable women, and it is no wonder that Antoine Nivon was smitten by her exotic looks and intelligence.

Another woman merchant and beauty, Juana Catarina Romero, was born in nearby Tehuantepec in 1837, just a year before young Antoine and Anastacia first met. Her story is extraordinary, and it provides detail about the culture and lifestyle of southern Oaxaca during the midnineteenth century. Famous for her friendship and romance with Porfirio Díaz while he was governor and general captain of Tehuantepec and throughout his long presidency, Romero became a symbol of feminine independence for Oaxaca that endures today.

Her Zapotec parents were poor—her father worked in a factory that made napkins, and her mother kept house and rolled cigarettes that she sold in the local market. Juana Catarina never attended school; she did not know how to read or write until she was thirty years old. But she was clever, industrious, and very intuitive about the politics of the region.

When Díaz met her in 1858, she was only twenty years old, but her strategic thinking impressed him, and he often relied on her insights in the district he had been assigned to govern. With some assistance from her high-ranking friend, and her own hard work, Juana Catarina set up a small store in a rented house and began to sell textile *huipiles* that were woven in the nearby hills.

Juana Catarina Romero was an exotic beauty, but her intelligence, political savvy, and entrepreneurial spirit were the qualities that earned her the lifelong affection of Porfirio Díaz. (Photo source: Francie R. Chassen-López.)

By 1867, she had traveled to Europe to see what fabrics and related products were being manufactured there, and she began to import muslin from England and silk thread from Austria, ensuring that the "traditional" dress items she produced were different from all the others. She designed a very special *sombrero* for men who wanted something unique in their wardrobe, and built a factory to manufacture "*Charros 24*"—hats made from German fabric and inlaid with silver that sold for twenty-four *duros*.

Like the Nivons, she produced anil dye, as well as cacao, and transported them by mule over the Sierra Madre mountains to Oaxaca City for export to Mexico City and Europe. And from the state's capital, she brought back special products for her store in the isthmus, items that could not be found in any other shop in the region. The round-trip one-thousand-kilometer journey meant travel along dirt roads—and sometimes no roads—through a landscape of cliffs and valleys, thick cactus and brush that protected snakes and jaguars, and only a very few primitive pueblos where she and her small caravan might find temporary shelter.

Romero helped establish the first branch of *Banco Nacional de México* in Tehuantepec, and she became the owner of the Santa Teresa Ranch by acquiring many small properties and combining them. Realizing that the advent of synthetic dyes would eventually ruin her thriving anil business, she traveled to Havana, Cuba, to study the sugarcane industry; soon she was producing this new crop with great success, with plans to expand into the production of syrup and rum.

Just as Romero had anticipated, the invention of synthetic dyes had a cataclysmic effect on Oaxaca's natural dye industry and on the Nivon fortunes. The prices for the beautiful natural dyes manufactured at Santa Yfigenia fell sharply, to a level below production cost. Merchants and landowners looked frantically for alternate crops, and estate peons turned to subsistence farming for themselves and their *hacendados*.

As the new emperor and empress continued to beautify their palace and magnificent gardens at Chapultepec in Mexico City, to design their opulent country retreat at Cuernavaca, and to build museums to showcase Mexican culture, there was growing concern about the extravagance of the rulers, especially as poverty, illiteracy, and even starvation were challenging the country's general population.

Maximiliano and Carlota were not oblivious to the plight of their Mexican subjects, and despite their lavish spending, they realized with shock that the gap between rich and poor citizens was far greater than they had imagined, that civil war still raged despite Napoleon III's reassurances that a favorable plebiscite existed, and that Mexico's finances were in chaos, worsened by the fact that Maximiliano had incurred large new debts to France for troops.

As quickly as possible the new emperor tried to implement reforms that would alleviate some of the problems. His diaries reflect a man who wanted to be a heroic figure, a ruler for the people. He abolished child labor, cancelled all debts over ten pesos for peasants, restored communal property, forbade capital punishment, and broke the monopoly of hacienda stores. Napoleon III was furious; Maximiliano had not become the "puppet" for France as planned, and before many of the new reforms could be put into effect, Napoleon III withdrew French troops from Mexico in 1865, leaving Maximiliano unprotected as the United States ended its civil war and prepared to help the ousted president Juárez. In a desperate effort to thwart disaster, Carlota left for Europe to confront Napoleon and urge him to honor his promise to her husband.

While Maximiliano and Carlota spent lavishly on their palace and gardens and built new museums to showcase Mexican culture, the country's general population was struggling. (Illustration source: Brown Brothers)

She was not in time. In 1867, Maximiliano went to Querétaro with eight thousand loyalist troops to fight the Juaristas. His betrayal by Colonel López is legendary, and he was condemned to death along with his generals Mejía and Miramón. International pleas for leniency were ignored, and Benito Juárez, restored as president, chose not to spare the Austrian. He was executed by a firing squad on June 19, at Cerro de las Campañas. His last words were spoken in Spanish:

> "I forgive everyone and I ask everyone to forgive me.
> May the blood that is about to be shed be for the good
> of the country. *Viva México, viva la independencia*."

His body was returned to Austria aboard the same ship that had brought him to Mexico with such fanfare just a few years before. Still in Europe, Carlota went insane and lived for the next sixty years in Belgium and Italy, apparently never knowing of her husband's death in Mexico. The short reign of the doomed monarchs became a story that would be told forever, all over the world.

Meanwhile, throughout Mexico the focus was on the upcoming presidential election scheduled for October. Political intrigue had reached a fever pitch, with Benito Juárez pushing for reelection and his rival, Porfirio Díaz, secretly and not-so-secretly trying to rally support for his own election. Since both contenders were from Oaxaca, the tension was especially felt in "the state of the Patriots."

Juárez was a Zapotec Indian, born in the Oaxacan countryside in 1806. As a little boy, he worked in the cornfields and as a shepherd, and spoke only Zapotec. When he was twelve years old, he walked to Oaxaca City and went to work as a servant, learning to speak and read Spanish. He attended church schools, since they were free, and eventually became a lawyer, judge, governor of Oaxaca, and president of Mexico.

Díaz's story, while somewhat different, has striking similarities. He was born in the city of Oaxaca on September 15, 1830, the evening before Mexican Independence Day. His ancestors were Spaniards, and his great-grandfather had married a Mixteca Indian, giving Díaz the claim that "in the veins of Don Porfirio is mixed the blood of the proudest provinces of Spain with that of the highest nations of America."

On June 19, 1867, restored President Benito Juárez ordered
the execution of Maximiliano by a firing squad at Cerro de las
Campañas. (Illustration source: General Bernardo Reyes, *El General
Porfirio Díaz*, J. Ballesca y Compañía, México, 1903)

His father, Don José Faustino Díaz, died of cholera in 1833, and the
family struggled financially. His mother, Doña Petrona Mory, ran an
inn to support the family; Díaz was educated in the local primary school
and entered the seminary when he was fourteen, that education being
free. A chance meeting with Benito Juárez, who was then governor of
Oaxaca, inspired the young man to study law, and four years later, after
Juárez's term as governor had expired, Díaz joined his law firm.

When President Santa Anna arrested and imprisoned Juárez, who
escaped to New Orleans, Díaz joined a small military band in the hills
of Oaxaca, fighting against the troops of Santa Anna. Military honors,
and the appreciation of Juárez upon his return to Mexico, paved
the way for Díaz to move up in the political hierarchy. From 1858
to 1860 he served as governor and general captain in Tehuantepec,
where he met Juana Catarina Romero, who urged him to build on his
increasing momentum. But with the momentum came competition
and rivalry.

As a little boy, Benito Juárez worked as a shepherd and a servant; he eventually became a lawyer, judge, governor of Oaxaca, and president of Mexico. (Photo source: General Bernardo Reyes, *El General Porfirio Díaz,* J. Ballesca y Compañía, México, 1903.)

As a young man, Porfirio Díaz was inspired by Benito Juárez, who was then governor of Oaxaca; his trajectory of political power began with military service in the hills. (Illustration source: General Bernardo Reyes, *El General Porfirio Díaz,* J. Ballesca y Compañía, México, 1903.)

On August 25, 1867, Juárez was feted at a banquet in Oaxaca, attended by most leaders of the Mexican government and the military, in celebration of the end of the French monarchy and the "Restored Republic." Instead of offering the traditional first toast, General Porfirio Díaz sat sullen and quiet. Finally, Juárez broke the tension by rising and toasting, "Liberty and Independence," breaking the uncomfortable silence that foreshadowed the years of bitter internal struggle between political factions that would follow.

In the October election, Díaz won the majority of votes in Oaxaca, with the important exception of the Sierra Zapoteca, and his control of the state was almost complete. But President Juárez easily won the majority of electoral votes in the rest of the country and was reelected. Of more immediate concern to the Nivon family, and to everyone else living in the isthmus region of Oaxaca, was the increasing dissatisfaction of the indigenous groups there. Their struggles to defend their *usos y costumbres* demonstrated the growing strength of ethnic and multiethnic identity; and the next decades were marked by battles over communal lands, new tax laws, and even what clothes could be worn in the larger towns of Oaxaca.

Don Antonio and Doña Anastacia Nivon, like other landowners in the isthmus, avoided direct involvement in politics; they watched with growing concern as Santa Yfigenia failed to find an alternate crop to their plummeting natural dye industry. Their children were all educated, fluent in Spanish, French, and Zapotec, accustomed to traveling abroad and to all the comforts of the hacienda life. Several daughters had married Europeans, following the precedent set by their mother, and the sons attempted to run the ranching operation, shifting to cattle raising and growing mangoes. These were difficult years for the next generation of Nivons; the young adults had not been prepared for the unexpected change in lifestyle. Hoping to assist this next generation with their new endeavors, Don Antonio divided the lands of Santa Yfigenia among nine of his children; and he and Anastacia retained the hacienda and a few hundred acres surrounding it.

Don Antonio and Doña Anastacia Nivon were one of the most respected
couples in the region, despite their decline in fortune following the
advent of synthetic dyes. Their portraits hung in the beautiful entry hall
of the Santa Yfigenia hacienda. (Photo source: Family collection.)

Federico went on to study law in the city of Oaxaca, at the Instituto
de Ciencias y Artes. Considered to be the most influential college
in nineteenth-century Mexico, it was where both Benito Juárez and
Porfirio Díaz studied, located near the *zócalo* where Juárez held an early
rally to call for the ousting of former president Santa Anna.

In 1875, the young lawyer married eighteen-year-old Gertrudis
Petriz, who had grown up in Tehuantepec, not far from Doña Juana
Cata Romero's state-of-the-art store near the *Palacio Nacional*. They
moved to a small farm in the neighboring Juchitán region and produced
a variety of crops that were sold in local markets. The nearby city of
Juchitán had a population of ten thousand, mainly speakers of Zapotec,
modern dirt streets, a new *zócalo*, and whitewashed government
buildings, storefronts, small offices, and a cathedral. Plans were under
way to build a small hospital and a government-run "normal school"
in the near future.

Gertudis Petriz was part of a prominent political family from Tehuantepec; she married Federico Nivon in 1875. (Photo source: Family collection.)

As Don Antonio's children grew up and established their own homes, they remained in four neighboring villages of the isthmus—Tehuantepec, Juchitán, Zanatepec, and Tapanatepec—and they always gathered at Santa Yfigenia for feast days and other celebrations.

Despite the decline in the Nivon fortune, the hacienda remained a haven, filled with books, music, and delicious meals, although now they came directly from the estate's own fields. In the grand entry hall, two large portraits of the hacienda's patriarch and matriarch kept watch over Santa Yfigenia—Don Antonio, with his blue eyes and handsome features, and Doña Anastacia, reflecting all the strength and beauty that the isthmus was known for.

Guadalupe's older sister Josefina was born in 1883 and was the
ninth child of Federico and Gertudis Nivon; the sisters remained
close for their entire lives. (Photo source: Family collection.)

Before he died in 1881, Don Antonio had welcomed dozens of
grandchildren, but he did not live to meet Federico's tenth child, little
María Guadalupe Nivon, born on December 12, 1885. Everyone agreed
he would have been delighted that this tiny granddaughter was born on
the same day as the Virgin of Guadalupe, the patron saint of Mexico.
Her soft brown curls and huge eyes hinted at the rare beauty that would
one day be hers, and it was clear to everyone who saw her and held her
that someone very special had entered the world.

All of the children born to Federico and Gertrudis Nivon were
taught to be entrepreneurial, following a pattern set long ago by both
the Fuentes and Nivon families. Guadalupe's sister, Josefina, was just
two years older, and by the time she was seven years old, she was riding
horseback through the isthmus, helping their father sell the goods he
brought to Mexico from Europe. Doña Anastacia had done the same

thing two generations ago, when Oaxaca enjoyed some of the most robust trade in Mexico.

But the world in Oaxaca was a tumultuous one. The widowed Doña Anastacia remained at Santa Yfigenia with her youngest child, Luis, who had been born in 1862. Don Antonio's happy guess during their vacation in La Drôme had been correct, and their last child had been born the following year. Now twenty-three years old, Luis had recently married, and his wife and new baby son, Carlos, lived at the family estate. The peons remained in large numbers, sustaining themselves and the Nivons with their cultivation of the land in lieu of commercial crops. Despite the erosion of its commercial viability, Santa Yfigenia's social prominence and territorial extension remained largely intact, truly remarkable considering the confiscations and devastations of the era. It was not until after the agrarian reform that followed the Mexican Revolution that the hacienda suffered major loss of property.

But the difficult economic times took a toll on the Nivon lifestyle. After Guadalupe's birth, Federico and Gertrudis had two more babies. Gertrudis did not survive her last childbirth; and the baby also died. Eleven youngsters proved too challenging for the widower, and when Guadalupe was five years old, Federico sent her to live with her widowed aunt Josefina in Tapanatepec, and he sent her younger brother to another relative. She attended the local convent school, learning French and English in addition to her native Spanish, needlepoint, music, and literature.

Located in the far south of Oaxaca near the Chiapas border, Tapanatepec was just a few miles from Santa Yfigenia, and several Nivon family members had beautiful homes surrounding the *zócalo* in the heart of town. White stucco with dark wooden beams, the houses were built in the traditional style of the times, with deep patios and gardens in the back. Cousins romped together from house to house, and despite a changing Mexico, there was a sense of security in the comfortable enclave where everyone was part of a large family, with branches stretching all over the isthmus.

Census records in the mid-1800s documented that members of
the large Fuentes and Nivon families were living throughout the
Isthmus of Tehuantepec. (Photo source: Family collection.)

Josefina Nivon had also taken in nine-year-old Antonia Casteneira,
whose family had fallen on hard times as well, and Guadalupe loved
having a "big sister" to play with and emulate. A gentle woman who
had always wanted a daughter, Josefina adored her two charges and
showered them with all the love and attention of a mother. Guadalupe's
thick chestnut-colored hair was always immaculately brushed and
braided, and when not in her school uniform, she was dressed with the
same style that had graced the Nivon family during their wealthier days.
The little girl's memories of another *mamá* were shadowy and faded with
time, and Guadalupe eventually came to believe that her aunt was her
mother.

When Guadalupe was eleven years old, her father arrived at the
house in Tapanatepec, shaken by frightening events that were taking
place in the Juchitán region. More than a thousand Chatino Indians

The Zapotecs were much admired as farmers and traders;
and they were known for their colorful traditional attire and
head coverings. (Photo source: Family collection.)

had attacked the district capital of Juquila, near the coast, protesting
against a new tax law, shouting, "Death to all who wear pants." They
struck out violently against the *gente decente* (whites and mestizos
dressed in European garb), burning the town hall and judicial archives,
and beheading twenty-two townspeople, among them two judges, the
jefe político, the municipal president, and other officials. The rebels
were communicating with other Chatino communities, urging them
to join in the extermination of all the *catrines* (fancy dressers). Oaxacan
Governor Martín González had dispatched the army's Fourth Battalion,
and violent fighting was under way.

It took nearly two weeks to recapture Juquila, and many Indians were executed or sent to Quintana Roo, Mexico's tropical Siberia. The governor appointed lawyer Carlos Woolrich, one of Federico Nivon's classmates at the *Instituto*, as Juquila's new *jefe político*. He decreed that anyone entering a town under his jurisdiction was forbidden to wear indigenous dress. *Huipiles* (women's blouses) and *camisa y calzón de manta* (rough cotton tops and bottoms for men) would no longer be tolerated. Everyone had to dress in European style or be punished. The ruling spawned a new enterprise: merchants set up stands at town entrances to rent shoes, jackets, and pants to Indians going to market.

Hearing the story, Guadalupe knew that grown-ups referred to the rebellion as "The War of the Pants," and despite agreeing on the tragedy of lives lost, they also shared laughter over the flexibility of the Indians, who now donned European clothes to enter markets and put on their own native clothing to go home to their villages and fields. The little girl wondered about the deepest thoughts of the peons who still worked the land at her grandparents' estate. Since she was fluent in Zapotec, she decided to ask them next time she traveled there.

Guadalupe was proud of her heritage, and she enjoyed talking to the locals of Santa Yfigenia, smiling at the stories they told her about the glory days of the estate when the Nivons "sunbathed the money" in their courtyard. When she asked her grandmother what they meant, Doña Anastacia explained that servants used to polish and dry the silver in the sunlight of the courtyard to counteract the tarnish and mineral deposits that blighted silver in the tropics.

Visits to Santa Yfigenia were special, although not as frequent as before. The grand piano would come to life as Guadalupe practiced her music, and her grandmother was proud of her growing proficiency at needlepoint, encouraging her to work on two kneeling pillows that would, in the Nivon tradition, someday be used at her own wedding in the cathedral. Doña Anastacia's eyes misted with tears, remembering her own wedding to Don Antonio Nivon nearly sixty years ago.

Everyone who came to Santa Yfigenia visited the small private cemetery not far from the house, where Don Antonio's tombstone stood in the shade of a mimosa tree:

Aquí yace	*Here lies*
Antonio Nivon	*Antonio Nivon*
Nació en Peyrus, Francia	*Born in Peyrus France*
El 14 de enero de 1811	*January 14, 1811*
Falleció en Tonala	*Died in Tonala*
El 7 de febrero 1881	*On February 7, 1881*
Dejando a su esposa	*Leaving his wife*
Y sus hijos	*And his children*
La mas profunda aflición	*The deepest sorrow*
Una plegariá por su alma	*A prayer for his soul*
Seale la tierra leve	*May the earth rest lightly upon him*

Don Antonio Nivon was buried in 1881 at his beloved
Santa Yfigenia. (Photo source: Family collection.)

Though remote in the nineteenth century, the Isthmus of Tehuantepec had been home to Antoine Nivon. It attracted the attention of kings, entrepreneurs, and adventurers, who all schemed to profit there. Don Antonio was captivated by it when he first crossed the mountains from Veracruz, not daunted by the steep cliffs and thick forests that gave way to a landscape of cactus, banana groves, and palm trees. He fell in love with a strong, beautiful native woman from the isthmus, and he built her a magnificent manor house with grand double arches, Italian marble, courtyards, patios, and gardens; a carpenter traveled from France to build its furniture and unique woodwork.

In the mid-1800s, Santa Yfigenia was a magnificent hacienda in southern Oaxaca; its carpentry was done by French artisans, and its furnishings included a grand piano and beautiful antique furniture from Europe. By the turn of the century, its grandeur had faded, but it remained the vibrant meeting place for the Fuentes and Nivon descendents living throughout the state. (Photograph of historic ruins of Santa Yfigenia; Family collection)

As the nineteenth century ended, Guadalupe Nivon had blossomed into an extraordinary beauty and had met her own handsome, dashing

European. They had told each other long and complicated stories of adventure, successes, and losses, and they had shared their daring dreams for the future. Not long after the Christmas holidays at Santa Yfigenia in 1902 they announced their engagement; they would begin their own new dynasty as the new century began.

"My grandfather had died a few years before we visited Aunt Helena in Mexico, where she was living on the Nivon family ranch north of Salina Cruz. One day we went by flatbed truck to a little village on the coast. We parked on the outskirts of the village, walking past adobe houses to a hillside overlooking a pristine cove. We saw a wooden fishing boat coming in to shore, and we all ran down to the water and jumped in with wild abandon, even the grown-ups. As the day ended all of the villagers came down to the beach to help pull in the fishermen's nets, and our family joined them. I remember standing by my father and feeling such joy that we were all doing this together. Suddenly I saw the bountiful catch in the heavy nets—large fish, silver and shining, sparkler-like as they refelcted the orange-red color of the setting sun. When we returned to the ranch at dark, all the laterns had been lit, and we ate dinner under the stars, celebrating our last night at the mountain and paying our respects to my grandfather."

John George "Sandy" McNab
Grandson of Guadalupe and John George McNab

Chapter 5

The Thistle and the Rose

Mexico: 1904–10

Guadalupe Nivon completed the last stitch of the kneeling pillow, an intricate work of needlepoint that she had designed in the delicate hues of Scottish heather, with a touch of the traditional McNab plaid. It was a beautiful complement to her own kneeling pad, created during her late teens, resplendent with red roses to commemorate her patron saint, the Virgin of Guadalupe. Both would soon be placed at the altar of Tapanatepec's cathedral; the Nivon-McNab nuptials were just one week away.

Her white lace dress had come from Paris, and for luck, she planned to wear the same pearls, inherited from her great-grandmother, she wore when she first met John George McNab. Considered the most beautiful woman on the isthmus, nineteen-year-old Guadalupe had blossomed like the roses on the kneeling pillow, yet she possessed a modesty and integrity that honored her namesake.

Despite their waning financial situation, the Nivon family prepared Santa Yfigenia for a grand celebration. Peasants who had worked there for years gladly returned to ready the mansion, polishing its furniture to a brilliance, once again "sunbathing" the silver platters that would hold carefully prepared delicacies that came straight from the estate's fields.

McNab's family in Illinois sent gifts and congratulations but could not make the four-week journey by train and carriage to the remote isthmus. From the Nivon family, aunts and uncles, siblings and cousins came from both the Tehuantepec and Juchitán regions, and from as

When Guadalupe Fuentes Nivon married John George McNab
in 1904, she was considered the most beautiful young woman
on the isthmus. (Photo source: Family collection.)

far away as Veracruz, to attend the wedding and to see Santa Yfigenia
restored to full glory for the occasion.

As Guadalupe prepared for her nuptials, she told her family's oldest
servant how much she wished her mother were alive, remembering the
special love she always felt in her home in Tapana. Deciding it was the
right time, as the old woman helped arrange Guadalupe's hair, she told
her that her mother, Gertrudis, had died when Guadalupe was barely
three years old, and that the woman she'd known as her *mamacita*
was actually her aunt. A family secret had been told, and suddenly,
some of the mysteries that shadowed Guadalupe's childhood memories
were resolved. Her eyes misted as she thought about her real mother,
long dead, her aunt, just recently placed in the family cemetery, and
her remarkable grandmother Doña Anastacia, who would be at the
cathedral to see the kneeling pillows put to use at last.

Many of McNab's colleagues from S. Pearson & Son were in the
cathedral as well, and John Body served as best man. Federico Nivon

walked his daughter down the ornate central aisle of the cathedral, which was lit with candles on every pew, to the altar where the priest and John George waited to receive her. The kneeling pillows were already placed at the railing, for the ceremony that would unite a "thistle" from Scotland and a "rose" from Mexico.

Soon after they were married, John George surprised his bride with a new home in Salina Cruz, the Oaxaca port which was the termination point of the new Tehauntepec Railroad that was being constructed under his supervision. The ocean breezes from the Pacific provided relief from the otherwise humid climate, and the couple enjoyed spending time in "the townhouse" whenever they weren't at the ranch properties that the Nivons had held for decades, to the north and south of Salina Cruz. Always an avid reader, John George filled the library with the classics of literature, and Guadalupe's beloved piano was moved from Santa Yfigenia to the elegant parlor.

The new home in Salina Cruz was elegant by 1904 standards, with a view of the port, lush gardens, and a library where McNab read original editions of poetry by John Keats and Robert Burns, but it did not have running water. (Photo source: Family collection.)

The Santa Gertrudis ranch was primitive, but McNab enjoyed hunting there and was known to be a crack shot. (Photo source: Family collection.)

The northern ranch was large, some forty thousand acres, and although the ancient stone mansion that had once stood on the highest hill had become a ruin over the last decades, a primitive "hunting camp" provided rough accommodations. Another of Guadalupe's older sisters, named Gertrudis in honor of their mother, had married a farmer named Pablo Ortega; together they ran the Nivon family's diminished cattle operation, sometimes living in Salina Cruz and sometimes on the ranch in the remote mountains to the north. Traveling to the ranch was not easy and included crossing a river on mules, but McNab enjoyed hunting there and often took colleagues from the Pearson Company to shoot birds, ocelots, and jaguars.

Despite the setbacks of the hurricane and earthquake two years earlier, the railroad project was nearing completion, and Pearson had requested McNab's participation in several new projects in other parts of Mexico.

In the early days of planning the Tehuantepec Railroad, John Body had learned from the natives that there was oil seepage in the isthmus. While locating rock that would be suitable for reinforcing the port works in Coatzacoalcos, Body had taken local workers with him to clear

Gertrudis "Tula" Nivon married Pablo Ortega; together they made the Santa Gertrudis a working cattle ranch in the early twentieth century. (Photo source: Family collection.)

the trail. Near San Cristóbal, he saw that the rock had oil nodes in it; the natives offered to show him the seepage.

The sludgy oil and tar that surfaced from underground had long been used by local people for waterproofing; and Body was told that it was plentiful. Excited, he passed the information along to Pearson, who was visiting Mexico in 1901. Aware of the oil boom occurring in Texas following the discovery of the huge Spindletop field, Pearson decided to investigate further. He realized that if he could find a good oil supply on the isthmus, he would have a wonderful solution to his problem of providing enough fuel for the locomotives and machine facilities that were part of the railroad project.

The company's current use of wood for fuel meant cutting down trees, requiring massive labor, which was scarce; and the hot cinders that flew from wood fuel caused damage to the sugar plantations and other agricultural enterprises along the rail line, raising costs and embittering

While working on the Tehuantepec Railroad project, John Body
and McNab learned from local laborers of oil seepage and reported
the news to Pearson. (Photo source: Family collection.)

relations with the local elites. Oil could provide Pearson with the sort
of creative solution he was known for worldwide.

His ideas were confirmed on his return journey to London. Traveling
by train from Mexico, he missed his connection in Laredo, Texas, and
decided to take advantage of this piece of "bad luck" by investigating
the burgeoning oil business in that state. He quickly observed the race
to buy and sell land for oil leases, and within a few hours, Pearson sent
Body an important cable, instructing him to buy "all land for miles
around." He advised his trusted employee to secure as much land as he
could in the vicinity of the seepage, and he sent the man who had put
down the first well at Spindletop to take a look at the subvention lands
in Pédregal and San Cristóbal. In a more detailed letter, dated April
19, 1901, written on stationery from the elegant Menger Hotel in San
Antonio, he explained that "oil deposits frequently extend over big areas,
so the oil rights must extend over a large district to be really valuable.

Ten, twenty, or forty thousand acres appears to be no uncommon size— so in getting the option, get it over as big a country as possible. A short option is no good. We must have it for a year at least—preferably two, as it would take time to put down an oil well or otherwise prove it."

For the next five years, Pearson quietly acquired controlling interests and properties in oil-rich areas throughout Mexico, and began bringing in small fields. Betting on big oil discoveries, he invested in refining and transportation facilities, pipelines, and port facilities. Body and McNab carried out his ventures with discretion and efficiency; they were confident that Pearson's two major endeavors would yield successful results: the Tehuantepec Railroad was nearing completion, and construction of the first experimental oil refinery to ascertain the best method for refining Mexican crude was under way.

John Body enlisted the help of his best Pearson team members, like John George McNab (on right), as he bought and leased land for "the Chief," Sir Weetman Pearson. (Photo source: Family collection.)

There were more personal reasons for celebration as well. John George and Guadalupe were overjoyed when their first child, a beautiful baby girl, was born in 1906. They named her Helena, the Spanish derivative honoring the many Helens in the Scottish ancestry of the McNab family. The following year, baby Estella was born; her father immediately nicknamed her *Neñeca*, his own made-up word that probably was meant to combine *niña* and *muñeca*, because she reminded him of a delicate doll. The townhouse echoed with the joyful sounds of babies and of music from Guadalupe's ebony piano. Servants were plentiful to help care for two babies, to cook for festive occasions that Guadalupe loved to plan, to clean and do laundry, and to help Guadalupe maintain the colorful gardens that were always blooming, enhanced by almost constant sunshine and humidity. Life was good for the McNabs.

Helena and Estella McNab, circa 1909, had more than one hundred Fuentes and Nivon cousins in the isthmus region. They played in the countryside, and sometimes they dressed up in the European tradition. (Photo source: Family collection.)

On the other hand, Sir Weetman Pearson was not experiencing much joy as the end of 1907 approached. Test drilling for oil had not produced significant results; now he needed some revenue to offset the cost of the idle infrastructure he had accumulated. For solace, he shifted his thoughts to the upcoming inaugural ceremonies for the new railroad project, which he considered to be his firm's greatest technical achievement to date.

The Tehuantepec Railroad project took a decade to build, connecting the Atlantic and Pacific oceans with slightly more than one hundred miles of track. (Photo source: Family collection.)

McNab had spent nearly ten years supervising the engineering and construction details, traveling through swampy regions where disease was rampant, and through rocky cliffs where dynamiting was the only way to penetrate the landscape for laying track. There had been delicate political maneuvers as well when President Díaz asked that the route be altered slightly to pass directly in front of the new chalet he was building for his special friend Doña Juana Catarina Romero, who lived in Tehuantepec. That way, he could easily board the train after visiting her. The company had provided McNab with a camera, a marvel of technology in the early years of the twentieth century, and he documented the building of the railroad with pride, sure that someday the challenges he and his team faced would be remembered and admired.

Just a few months before little Estella McNab's birth, citizens of the isthmus witnessed a spectacular public celebration, the completion of the long-awaited first journey of the Tehuantepec Railroad. Four special railroad cars made the trip from Mexico City traveling west on the railroad to Veracruz then south to the isthmus, where a vision more than three hundred years old would become a reality. Newspapers and newsreels around the world covered the opening of the new railroad, sharing maps of the route and predicting the impact it would have on international trade. The train's progress across the isthmus provided drama and excitement throughout Mexico and beyond.

President Porfirio Díaz traveled in the second car with his cabinet and Sir Weetman Pearson; John Body and the diplomatic corps rode in an accompanying car, the "Thompsoniana," property of the US ambassador, David E. Thompson. When they arrived at the Santa Lucrecia station of the Veracruz and Isthmian Railway, they were greeted by a huge, newly built arch that proclaimed: "Mexican Isthmian Route, the World's Commercial Bridge … fulfilled by the far-seeing energy of General Díaz and his government."

After Santa Lucrecia, the train began a steep climb to enter the Malatengo Canyon, where the route had been blasted directly through rock and chasms to arrive at Rincón Antonio. Here the Pearson Company had created a modern British-style town, populated totally by the railroad company and its employees. Next, the train went through the Chivela Pass, the highest point on the track, a spot where travelers could view both oceans at the same time.

Sir Weetman Pearson addressed the crowds that had gathered in Salina Cruz, thanking first the president of Mexico for the opportunity to build the new railroad, and then acknowledging the extraordinary work of the Pearson team, led by John Body and John George McNab. He concluded by saying, "When your government, General Díaz, decided to undertake the gigantic enterprise that we are here today to inaugurate, I had the honor to be appointed the instrument to carry out the work of such magnitude of international importance, I need hardly say that such an expression of trust and confidence in my firm was most gratifying."

Preparations for the inaugural journey of the new railway were well-orchestrated, and reporters were expected from all over Mexico and beyond to witness the event. (Photo source: Family collection.)

President Díaz's reply expressed his happiness over the great achievement, which he characterized as a milepost in Mexican history. Surrounded by his entourage and members of the Oaxacan elite, the president pushed the button on the electric crane that lifted fifteen sacks of Hawaiian sugar from the ship *Arizona* onto the freight cars on the railroad. As the train began its trip to Puerto Mexico, the cheers of the crowd overpowered the local band's serenade, and the president laughed and waved.

In his presidential message later that year, Díaz announced that during the first five months of the railroad's operation, 123,000 tons of merchandise had crossed the isthmus. He predicted this would increase rapidly, and he was right. In 1907, sixty-seven ships were anchored in Salina Cruz; two years later this number had increased to ninety-six ships, and the increase in cargo transported was also considerable.

The new railroad passed within ten feet of the new home of Juana Cata Romero, Tehuantepec's leading businesswoman and Porfirio Díaz's good friend.

The Pearson Company received much-deserved praise for accomplishing what no one else had been able to do, despite the tremendous amount it cost to build the railroad. It had begun work on another railroad in Chihuahua, and its new oil ventures were deepening the company's already huge partnership with Mexico. Frederick Adams, the agent in charge of the Salina Cruz Harbour Works, and a vice president of S. Pearson and Son Sucesores, was preparing to retire with his wife and daughter in Xalapa, and he highly recommended John George McNab for his important position in the busy port.

President Porfirio Díaz proclaimed the building of the Tehuantepec Railroad a milepost in Mexico's history, and the enthusiastic crowds agreed. (Photo source: Wikimedia Commons/Public Domain.)

The port of Salina Cruz was a hub for shipping and commerce; and large vessels like these carried diverse products to and from Mexico. (Photo source: Family collection.)

As the agent in charge of *Obras del Puerto de Salina Cruz,* McNab ran the equivalent of the port authority for S. Pearson & Son, a huge undertaking given the rapid growth of the port's commerce. Days were spent overseeing this bustling enterprise, for which Pearson had negotiated a fifty-year contract with Mexico.

Following cultural tradition, he went home for formal afternoon meals with Guadalupe, taking delight in his baby daughters, grateful that their nanny took them to the nursery while he read the current newspapers at the huge mahogany desk in the library. Later in the afternoon, as Salina Cruz awakened from its *siesta,* McNab returned to his office near the long pier in the harbor, where he kept detailed records of all operations—from employee logs to ship logs and contents—which were sent weekly to John Body via a horse-drawn coach.

By 1908, the port of Salina Cruz was bustling—shipping goods to international ports, maintaining a busy shipyard, and managing hundreds of employees. (Photo source: Family collection.)

John Body often asked McNab to travel to Mexico City, where the company's main office in Mexico was located, and to Veracruz and

Tampico, where Pearson's floundering oil venture presented challenges for an engineer who was well-known for his troubleshooting skills. Transportation by horseback, stagecoach, and railroad was rough, and each option required stamina and endurance. McNab's travels sometimes lasted several weeks, and he was comforted by the fact that Guadalupe's large family was nearby. Most of her ten siblings had married; the number of cousins his daughters could play with could have populated a small village.

In March 1908, the Pearson Company opened a state-of-the-art refinery in Minatitlán, after several years of construction. Pearson approached Waters Pierce, hoping to negotiate an agreement to refine and ship their crude, but unsurprisingly, given his aggressive buildup of refinery capacity, it fell through. Finally, in June, the first large flowing well was struck. But the excitement was soon followed by disaster, when the strike caught fire and proved impossible to extinguish. The fire lasted for eight weeks and destroyed the entire field. Even someone with the depths of Pearson's pockets was beginning to doubt the wisdom of his enterprise, as he wrote after losing his first big field:

> "I entered lightly into the enterprise, not realising its many problems, but only feeling that oil meant a fortune and that hard work and application would bring satisfactory results. Now I know that it would have been wise to surround myself with proved oil men who could give advice that their past life showed could be relied on, and not, as I did, relied upon commercial knowledge and hard work coupled with a superficial knowledge of the trade."

In 1909, after another attempt to make a deal with Pierce, Pearson formed a separate company to take over the oil properties, with John Body at its helm. The following year, the first public issue of shares in the new *Compañía Mexicana de Petróleo El Aguila SA* took place. Weetman Pearson invited the *científicos*, technocrats given positions and concessions by President Díaz, to invest in the new venture, realizing that their support would be valuable in both financial and political ways. The governor of the Federal District, President Díaz's son, the president of the National Railways of Mexico, Mexico's secretary of foreign relations, and the mayor of Mexico City were among the first investors. Henry W. Taft, brother of the US president, and US Attorney General George W. Wickersham invested in the new oil company as well. Pearson's top management, including John Body and John George McNab, were given stock options too, in appreciation for their hard work, and as incentives for future success.

Registered in Mexico, with more than $80 million of Mexican capital, El Aguila enjoyed the political advantages of a Mexican company, and its secondary listing as Mexican Eagle gave Pearson a financial advantage on the London stock exchange without the limitations of stringent British reporting requirements.

At Pearson's request, John Body (left) and John George McNab (right) made personal visits—often on horseback—to the "científicos" of President Díaz's regime, offering them the first public shares of the new Petróleo El Aguila, S.A. (Photo source: Family collection.)

Through his New York law firm, Taft represented Pearson's railroad and oil holdings in Mexico, and Wickersham, a member of the same firm, was counsel for the bondholders in the reorganization of the National Railways of Mexico that resulted when Porfirio Díaz nationalized the industry not long after his famous ride across the isthmus.

As John George and Guadalupe watched the Tehauntepec Railway change hands, again with celebratory fanfare, they had another, personal, reason for excitement. Another baby was on the way, and in early 1909, their first son was born.

The parents were overjoyed, and named him John, in honor of his father and grandfather. Their joy was short-lived; John died in infancy, not long after his first birthday, joining the large number of children who were victims of the high rate of infant mortality in the disease-ridden tropics of the isthmus. As the sorrowful parents dismantled his nursery, they looked to the future, wondering if a move away from Salina Cruz and its health risks should be considered.

Pearson's spirits were also at a low point. His railroad now belonged to the Mexican government, and his oil gamble had not produced the results he had expected. Both Pearson and McNab were hopeful that the new year would bring change; but they never dreamed how big those changes would be.

In 1910, Pearson hired a twenty-four-year-old college student from Kansas to map the geological structure of the oil fields he was exploring. Everette Lee DeGolyer saw the oil business as a science rather than a game of chance, and his contributions to the El Aguila Company and the overall oil industry brought bigger changes in both technologies and fortunes than Pearson had ever imagined possible. Born in a sod hut near Greenburg, Kansas, in 1886, DeGolyer came from very humble beginnings, much like Pearson's own grandfather. He was a daring, resourceful scientist with a vivid, practical, inquisitive intelligence much like Pearson's. He arrived in Mexico grateful for a chance to work for the famous engineer/contractor, and he threw himself wholeheartedly into trying to turn around Pearson's rather dismal drilling record.

In 1910, Britain honored Pearson with a peerage, in recognition of the major role he had played in making his country the top industrial nation in the world. He became Baron Cowdray, choosing the name of his large estate in Sussex. (Photo source: Pearson Archive, Science Museum Library, Swindon, United Kingdom.)

In the autumn of 1910, DeGolyer selected a new location in Veracruz for drilling, and the massive Potrero #4 well gushed into existence on December 27. It took sixty days to cap it, yielding one hundred thousand barrels a day. Second in size only to Spindletop, during its eight-year life it produced more than one hundred million barrels of oil, and was the turning point in the company's fortunes.

DeGolyer worked as chief geologist for Mexican Eagle until 1916, when he returned to the United States to finish his college degree and became a consultant. A few years later, when Pearson sold his Mexican oil interests, he convinced his remarkable young protégé to organize a new oil company in California; they named it Amerada, and its success is legendary to this day. When DeGolyer died in 1956, he was a multimillionaire living in Dallas, Texas. He had been awarded many of the same scientific honors that were bestowed on Thomas Edison, Orville Wright, and Alexander Graham Bell, and was easily considered the most renowned petroleum geologist in the world.

A black leather diary, embossed in gold with Pearson's initials, dated 1910, contains the meticulous notes of the visionary engineer whose business empire in Mexico now included public utilities, manufacturing, transportation, urban and rural properties, and a huge oil venture. There is praise for young DeGolyer, as well as sketches of pipelines; maps have been pasted onto pages to illustrate Potrero, Tuxpan, Tanuijo, and Tancoachín; and careful notes about gravity, exhaust steam used for heating, and twenty-four-hour tests of boiler pressure are part of the notebook that today is one of the treasures in the Pearson Archive in the Science Museum Library in Wroughton, England.

A second, unmarked diary from the same year is alphabetized by topics and ideas that were on Pearson's uniquely creative mind. He included detailed notes and possible applications to current and future projects. For example, a few of Pearson's listings under the letter A include:

Ashes vs. land for mortar (page 24)
Allowance for bark on timber (page 63)
Australian ironbark logs (page 108)

Now in his midfifties, Pearson was legendary for his political and business acumen and for successful projects all over the world. The government of Great Britain recognized that he was largely responsible for the country's status as the top industrial nation in the world, and in 1910, Pearson received a peerage as the first Baron Cowdray. As is the custom, he was asked to choose the name that would be associated with his new title; he chose the name of the beautiful Cowdray Estate he owned in Sussex, in southern England.

He also had reached heroic stature within his own company; his younger protégés like John George McNab and Everette DeGolyer looked forward to his visits to their regions and to the opportunity to learn from such an inspiring mentor.

John Body, too, was much admired by McNab; their friendship would last for the rest of their lives, long after both had left Mexico for new adventures in Britain and the United States. Like Guadalupe, Body's wife was born in Mexico, and a deep love for the "Mexican mind and culture" was an integral part of the man who was described by all who knew him as *muy simpático*, "very nice," always a gentleman even in the most difficult of times.

And times were becoming more difficult by the day. During the

In the fall of 1910, government agents discovered that Francisco Madero had purchased fifty thousand rifles from an American arms factory, a clear indication that trouble was ahead. (Photo source: Robert Dorman, Bettmann/Corbis.)

presidency of Porfirio Díaz, Mexico did not enjoy rule of law. Instead, a coalition of key asset holders and the political elite provided stability to a country that had suffered terribly during the past era of frequent political coups and stationary banditry.

By encouraging his main political rivals, the regional political elites, to enter business activities that were dependent on his federal government, Díaz enlisted state governors to become part of the *Porfiriato* system rather than fomenters of revolution. The system worked as long as asset values continued to rise, and foreign investments of capital and expertise by companies like S. Pearson and Son helped make that possible.

Mexican historians note that during Díaz's presidency foreign investors poured more than $2 billion into Mexico. Each of the major investors had a representative like John Body, someone who was fluent in Spanish, culturally sensitive, and well connected to the right political forces.

By 1910, the earlier whispers about the political ideals and ambitions of an intellectual named Francisco Madero had turned to shouts, especially in Mexico's northern states. His promises to author a new constitution and to return lands to the poor were the harbingers of revolution. As they rejoiced at Pearson's first big discovery of oil in Mexico, and the potential fortune located just beneath the surface of those lands, Body and McNab both recognized that a "new system" was almost certain to emerge in the near future. They hoped the love they felt for their adopted country, and the resilience of its people, would prove strong enough to meet that new future with courage and adaptability.

John George McNab (man in hat, closest to derrick) was on the scene when the El Potrero #4 gushed into existence as the second-largest oil well in the world. (Photo source: Family collection.)

"His dark eyes peered intently at the baby's bright blue eyes; his rough riding glove stroked her remarkable red hair. Pancho Villa was so mesmerized by this encounter in the desert of Chihuahua that he made a most unusual decision, luckily for us."

McNab family story
documented by letter from Pancho Villa, 1911

Chapter 6

The Red-Haired Angel

Mexico: 1910–15

As Pearson watched the huge plumes of black smoke fill the skies of Tuxpam, in the state of Veracruz, other entrepreneurs, financiers, and emerging oil barons around the world were watching too, hopeful that it was not too late to participate in this newest opportunity to build fortunes abroad. American E. L. Doheny already was operating oil fields near Tampico, and his Huasteca Petroleum Company quickly started new drilling farther south, not far from the El Potrero gusher.

Well known for his unique combination of imagination and engineering expertise, Pearson also had valuable political skills; he clearly understood how to operate within the *Porfiriato* system. As a result of the many confidential reports he received from people in high political positions in Mexico, Great Britain, and the United States, and from his own special intuition about power and politics, Pearson made a well-calculated move in 1910 when he selected a president for El Aguila Oil.

Enrique Creel was a wealthy rancher, banker, and businessman in Chihuahua, and was someone Pearson knew and trusted. He was married to Angela Terrazas, who came from an equally prominent family in northern Mexico, and was his first cousin. Their mothers were the beautiful Cuilty sisters: Paz had married a wealthy American consul named Ruben W. Creel, and Carolina had married Don Luis Terrazas, one of Chihuahua's largest landowners.

When the second-largest oil well in the world gushed into existence
in Mexico, foreign investors rushed to the scene in pursuit of
new opportunity. (Photo source: Family collection.)

After their children married and created the Terrazas-Creel clan,
their combined land holdings were more than 8.7 million acres in
Chihuahua, and the extended family owned mines, granaries, textile
mills, railroads, telephone companies, haciendas, and ranches. Estimates
put the family's net worth at more than $69 million prior to the
revolution.

A close friend of Porfirio Díaz, Creel was appointed by the president to the National Mexican Company of Dynamite and Explosives, along with Díaz's son, Porfirio Jr., and the treasury minister's son, Julio Limantour. This was an especially important, powerful appointment, since dynamite and explosives were in huge demand in Mexico during the boom in railroad construction and mining prior to the revolution. By imposing an 80 percent import tariff on dynamite, they quickly monopolized the market, and Creel used his wealth and connections to bolster commerce in his state and beyond.

In 1910, the hacienda system was deeply ensconced in northern Mexico; one of the largest operations belonged to the Terrazas-Creel family, which was involved in ranching, mining, textiles, railroads, utilities, and now oil. (Photo source: Brown Brothers.)

Envisioning the growth in business and industry that could occur if there was a working railroad, Creel became involved in railway projects in the mid-1800s, when Chihuahua had approximately 750 miles of track.

By 1900, there were more than twelve thousand miles of track, and as domestic markets expanded, raw materials could be transported, and there was new integration of workers along the Mexico-United States border. By 1902, he was vice president of the Chihuahua-Pacific Railroad and the Kansas City Railroad; and he was very much aware of the railroad being built in southern Mexico by S. Pearson & Son that would soon connect the Atlantic and Pacific oceans.

In 1904, Creel was elected governor of Chihuahua, succeeding his father-in-law, Don Julio Terrazas. In his zest for increased international commerce, Creel introduced new laws that permitted the sale of underutilized community land to outsiders, and land transfers in Chihuahua increased at a startling speed over the next few years. With an eye on growing railroad activity in the north, Pearson took advantage of the new laws, adding a large parcel of land to his already vast holdings in Mexico.

Pearson and Creel became good friends, and the Mexican governor met often with Pearson's director of Mexico operations, John Body, knowing that he represented the Pearson Company in every venture as the man "in charge" in Mexico. Body encouraged Creel to utilize his company's engineering expertise on railroad and other construction projects in Chihuahua, describing the efficiency and dedication of the Pearson team. He often praised a Scotsman named John George McNab, who would soon complete the massive railroad project in the isthmus that had captured Creel's attention a few years before. In conversation, Body suggested that McNab eventually might be available to come to northern Mexico as a troubleshooter for Creel's own railroad project.

The state of Chihuahua was an early hotbed of revolutionary
activity. (Photo source: Family collection.)

As the first decade of the twentieth century drew to a close, ominous
signs of change were discernible, even as new businesses boomed and
infrastructure grew. Northern Mexico was the first to feel the rumblings
of a discontented population. By 1908 many Chihuahua residents had
become landless laborers, and as work became harder and harder to find
on either side of the border, the state became a center for revolutionary
activity.

In 1909 President Díaz met with US President Taft, hoping to dispel
the rumors that Francisco Madero would be elected the following year.
Enrique Creel served as the translator during these sensitive discussions.
The following year, Creel was appointed secretary of foreign relations,
and not long after that, he received a disturbing telegram from the
Mexican consul in Galveston alerting him that Madero was building an
arsenal of guns and ammunition purchased in the United States.

MEXICAN TELEGRAPH COMPANY
VIA GALVESTON.

Comunicación rapida entre oficinas de la Compañia, Centro y Sud America, Los Estados Unidos y todas partes de Europa, etc.

Ciudad de Mexico, Avenida del Cinco de Mayo, 57.
Vera Cruz, Calle de la Independencia, No. 1.

Date

295   SANANTONIO TEXAS   21   KBW   XXNER

SENOR ENRIQUE C CREL SECRETARIO DF RFLACIONES
EXTERIORES MFX.

HOY MEDIO DIA LLEGO AQUI FRANCISCO MADERO PROCEDENTE LAREDO TEXAS
FUE ENCONTRABO   ESTACION POR SANCHEZ ASCONA ERNETO FERNANDEZ
SOSPEDASE CASA FERNANDES .

ENRIQUF ORNELAS.

10 20 PM B

LA RECTIFICACIÓN DE PALABRAS DUDOSAS, DEBERÁ SOLICITARSE POR MEDIACIÓN DE LA COMPANIA,
QUIEN SE ENCARCARA DE OBTENERLA SIN EXPENDIO ALGUNO.

Worries that Francisco Madero was building momentum were
confirmed when Enrique Creel received a telegram from the Mexican
consul in the United States alerting him of Madero's activities.
(Photo source: Secretaría de Relaciónes Externos, México.)

About the same time, Pearson asked Creel to serve as the first
president of the newly formed El Aguila Oil Company. He agreed to
accept a leadership role in this exciting new Pearson endeavor, confident
that it would be another success on a long list that included the recently
opened Tehuantepec National Railway. As Creel carefully watched the
developing political turmoil, he began to work with John Body to put
together a team for El Aguila that included engineers and geologists
from the United States. When Body suggested that John George McNab
could soon join him in Chihuahua to assist with Creel's railroad and
construction projects, as well as with the El Aguila venture, he was
delighted. Creel knew that McNab had most recently run the port at
Salina Cruz, was respected as a troubleshooter for the company, and that
his engineering and construction skills would be invaluable as Pearson
and Creel expanded the infrastructure of Chihuahua.

The move to Mexico's northern desert state was arduous for the McNab family, despite the accommodations of the Pearson Company's private railroad car. Traveling by train from the isthmus with Guadalupe (pregnant again and still grieving for little John), two toddlers, household staff, and luggage and furnishings for their new house was quite an undertaking. Current political unrest added tension to their journey northward; the McNabs would soon be in Madero's home territory, the epicenter of approaching trouble. The volcanic eruptions of Colima during the past year had been a sign of change from the natural world, and as the train passed through the villages of central Mexico, John George and Guadalupe observed firsthand the diverse faces and voices of a country in transition. What had been whispers about the challenges to President Díaz's authority had grown loud and gained momentum, churning and rattling much like the wheels of the train bound for its remote desert destination. From the train's windows, John George saw the first real evidence of violence; he struggled to keep the curtains drawn so Guadalupe and the children would not see it.

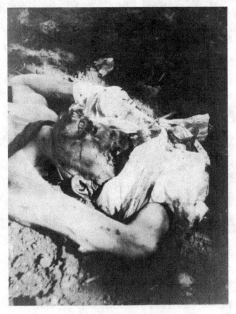

The roadsides of northern Mexico turned gruesome; burned corpses left little doubt that the revolution had begun. (Photo source: Family collection.)

Trying not to think about the scenes beyond the windows, John George turned his attention from the upcoming elections to the immediate work at hand in Chihuahua.

McNab knew the area well. The Thomson Ranch, where he had worked after graduating from the University of Wisconsin, had stretched from Eagle Pass into both Texas and northern Mexico. He was familiar with the dry air and the sand and alkali plains that dominate most of the land there, relieved only by scarce areas along the riverbanks and in the mountain valleys where the soil is fertile. Instead of the tropical vegetation he had become accustomed to in Oaxaca, he remembered the thorny, angular forms of *mezquite, tornilla, fouquiera, agave,* and *yuca* that grew wild. He wondered how Guadalupe and the girls would react to this strange new landscape. It was an escape from the humid climate of the tropics but an extreme one.

In Chihuahua, McNab supervised excavation projects for Pearson, in partnership with Enrique Creel. (Photo source: Family collection.)

Not long after the move to Chihuahua, the family welcomed its newest member, born in La Boquilla, on December 21, 1910. Her parents had planned to name her Isabel, but when John George saw her bright red hair, he wanted a name that captured her Scottish ancestry and suggested Flora. Guadalupe didn't like it, so they settled on Fiona, the Gaelic derivative of Flora. Her two older sisters, Helena and Estella, doted on the new baby, and her unique looks soon earned her the adoration of all the *locales*, eventually captivating even one of the most famous generals of the Mexican Revolution.

The family moved into a newly constructed "agent house," with a library and music room but still no running water. (Photo source: Family collection.)

Don Juan Jorge McNab stood on the wide porch of the ranch house, his blue eyes creased with worry. He squinted across the fields toward the mountains, seeing the familiar prickly pears jutting from the loose, dry soil, watching the families who farmed his land disappear inside the small adobe houses that bordered green swaths of alfalfa and cotton.

Puffs of red dust confirmed the warning his men had brought him just an hour ago, as his family was finishing an elaborate Sunday lunch of *crema de queso, frijoles charros, tortillas sobaqueras,* and *cabrito,* tender baby goat grilled over a wood fire, a specialty of northern Mexico.

Pancho Villa was approaching.

Just days before, Villa's *constitucionalistas* had taken control of Ciudad Chihuahua, only thirty miles away; now the merchants and wealthy citizens were abandoning the city, fearful of the general's reputation for violence.

Since the Terrazas-Creel family epitomized the hacienda system in northern Mexico, it was the root of vengeance for many revolutionaries. Villa's sweeps through the area already had expropriated a few banks and mines; the family and its holdings were very definite targets.

McNab buttoned his formal jacket in preparation for the inevitable meeting with the famous revolutionary fighter, described in the *New York Times* that was on the desk in the library as a former bandit who entered the Mexican Revolution with only a borrowed revolver, a man with a price on his head—volatile and dangerous.

Plumes of red dust announced a visit from legendary revolutionary Pancho Villa. (Photo source: Family collection.)

Stepping back inside the hacienda, McNab paused in the cool entryway, aware that Guadalupe and his three young daughters had begun to prepare for the afternoon siesta, aware also that the large cache of weapons and ammunition he kept hidden in an adjoining building could cost them all their lives.

Quite a horseman, Villa was thick-jawed with flicking animal eyes. He galloped into the McNab compound with a dozen members of his famous Dorado cavalry and ordered the men to search the hacienda and outbuildings for weapons, which "foreigners were not allowed to own."

As the bandit-turned-general stood on the porch of the hacienda with McNab, Guadalupe came to the doorway, holding her infant daughter, Fiona, surprised by the scene in front of her. Terror soon replaced her surprise when Francisco "Pancho" Villa asked to hold the baby.

His dark eyes peered intently at Fiona's bright blue ones; his rough riding glove stroked her remarkable hair. He was mesmerized by this tiny red-haired angel, and when his men reported that they had found weapons in one of the outbuildings, Villa made an unusual decision.

He announced that they were leaving the hacienda without taking any action, and insisted on giving McNab his personal guarantee of the family's safety. Entering the hacienda's library, Villa sat at the *hacendado's* desk and composed the note shown on the following page.

For the next two months, fighting in northern Mexico escalated, and Francisco Madero, who had slipped back into Mexico from the United States in February, had placed himself at the head of the revolution. The Díaz government, which strongly supported all of the Pearson projects, was crumbling. John Body kept Pearson updated through daily cable, and on May 18 he sent a letter filled with details from confidential sources, describing the historic events that would unfold during the next week in Mexico.

Violence was escalating throughout Mexico; human carnage reached the streets of the country's capital. (Photo source: Family collection.)

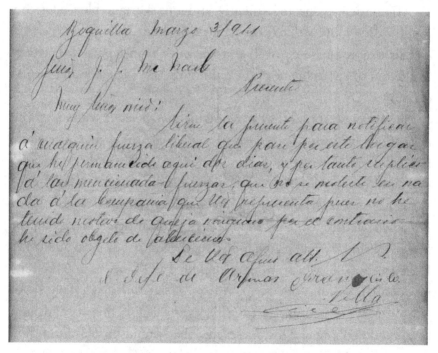

In a handwritten note, dated March 3, 1911, Pancho Villa extended protection to John George McNab and his family, largely because of Fiona's beautiful red hair. (Photo source: Family collection.)

The note reads:

Boquilla, March 3, 1911
Fino J. J. McNab

My dear friend:
The present letter serves to notify any liberal forces that pass through this place that I have stayed here two days and for that reason I request that said forces not bother in any way the Company which you represent given that I have had no complaint whatsoever; indeed on the contrary, I received many courtesies.

Pancho Villa

(By referring to McNab as "Fino," Villa accorded him
the status of gentleman; J. J. = Juan Jorge.)

Body reported that "an armistice was signed last night at eleven o'clock, and is for a period of five days, within which time it is expected that the President will resign and it is thought that Madero will come to Mexico and with the Minister of Foreign Affairs will form the new Cabinet ...

"The new Minister of War is to be General González Salas, who is quite well known to us ... a neutral man, and acceptable to both sides. The Minister of the Interior is to be Dr. Francisco Vázquez Gómez, Madero's Diplomatic Agent who was at Washington; and the Minister of Justice is to be Lic. Manuel Vázquez Tagle, a noted criminal lawyer."

The letter goes on to describe the intense anxiety and fear permeating Mexico City and beyond. Body reported that everyone expected mob violence, and threats to blow up bridges on railroad lines and cut transmission lines were rampant; only three thousand soldiers were posted in all of the Federal District, and its citizens were feeling totally vulnerable and were already witnessing violence in the streets.

Revolutionary forces blew up bridges on railroad lines and cut
transmission lines, and travel in Oaxaca could only be undertaken
on horseback. (Photo source: Family collection.)

Outside of the city, things were even worse. Travel in Oaxaca could
only be undertaken by horseback, since the rebels had control of the
southern railroad, and all telephonic communication to the Potrero
camp ended when the lines were cut.

Body adds, "The horrible remarks which have been made about
the President are too disgusting to write you, and there is a very bitter
feeling that is very general … there is a very '*triste*' and unsettled feeling
amongst all classes here, and business is practically at a stand-still, and
everyone who has been able to has got away from the country."

On May 25, Don Porfirio resigned. The next day he was escorted
to Veracruz by a grim-faced Indian general named Victoriano Huerta,
riding in comfort on John Body's own personal railroad car, and was
placed on the German ship *Ypiranga*, bound for exile in Europe.

Body sent a five-page letter to Lord Cowdray on May 27, describing
in detail "the secret departure from the City of the President," noting
that there was a great deal of criticism about his leaving without saying
good-bye to many of his friends and supporters.

Once President Díaz resigned and fled the country, Francisco Madero
assumed the presidency and set up his temporary cabinet in Juárez.
(Photo source: Augustín Victor Casasola, Archivo Casasola.)

Díaz and his party left San Lázaro station at four o'clock in the
morning on May 26, and it was not until noon that the general public
knew of his departure. Fred Adams, Pearson's vice president and former
agent in charge in Salina Cruz, was selected to travel to Veracruz on
an earlier train, on the pretext that he was traveling as the king's
messenger with dispatches from the legation in Mexico City to be
sent from Veracruz, since the cable line between the two cities had
been cut.

Confiding the intricate plan to Lord Cowdray, Body wrote:

> "It was anticipated that if Adams was held up he
> would be unmolested on account of carrying Foreign
> Government despatches and that he would have time to
> communicate with the train running behind to stop as
> he also had most full authority for all railroad employees
> to obey his orders in everything."

The plan worked, and Díaz made it safely to Veracruz, traveling on to Europe a few days later. "You can realize the relief it was to me when I had Adams' message yesterday over cable that they had arrived safely," Body concludes.

Now officially in charge, Madero established a temporary capital in Juárez and announced the names of his provisional cabinet. His uncle, Ernesto Madero, was given the portfolio of "Hacienda," and Lic. Rafael Hernández became the new minister of justice. Body reported to Lord Cowdray that he had served on the Mining Board with both men; he would begin the important, delicate political work he was known for as the new administration began.

Even though the revolution of 1911 would prove to be mild compared to what was to follow, it split the country asunder, and reports of violence and bloodshed spread via newspaper coverage and the new industry of the "photo postcard," offering a gruesome souvenir of the spectacle of revolution.

Intensely aware of the perilous situation in Chihuahua and many other parts of Mexico, the McNab family decided to return to Oaxaca, where relatives and friends provided a measure of stability in a world that was anything but stable. He and Guadalupe still shuddered at the memory of Pancho Villa holding Fiona, but they tried to focus on the happy diversions that their three daughters would enjoy when they returned to Salina Cruz and their extended family there. McNab knew that the family's respite in the tropical isthmus would be temporary and wondered where the company would next require his expertise and presence.

Meanwhile, El Aguila Oil Company continued its fast-paced growth in the states of Veracruz, Tabasco, Campeche, and Tamaulipas. Just months after Porfirio Díaz left Mexico, it built a pipeline from Potrero to Tuxpam, a distance of thirty miles, and then a much longer one to Tampico, one hundred miles away. The company now owned six tankers as well, giving it still more control over the petroleum industry. But because the tankers belonging to the Mexican Eagle Transport

Company were the largest in the world, with a capacity of one hundred thousand barrels of oil, they could not get into the shallow waters of Tampico's port for loading. After pondering this dilemma, Pearson designed an innovation that he called a "submarine pipeline," which made it possible to load tankers lying about a mile offshore, solving the problem of the shallow ports and revolutionizing the petroleum industry. Oil companies all over the world soon copied the submarine pipeline loaders.

In 1912, El Aguila Oil received its first big contract, committing to provide ten million barrels of crude to Standard Oil within five years. The same year, President Madero and his vice president, Pino Suárez, were "arrested" in Mexico City by General Huerta, who sent this message to President Taft in the United States: "I have the honor to inform you that I have overthrown this Government. The forces are with me, and from now on peace and prosperity will reign." Within a week Madero and Suárez were murdered under circumstances that pointed to Huerta; the world was shocked and horrified. In El Paso, Pancho Villa was grieved and enraged. Cautiously he collected modest funds, purchased arms and ammunition, and acquired some horses. On a dark night in April 1912, with only eight followers, he quietly crossed the Rio Grande. The real Mexican Revolution was just beginning.

Before the news of Pancho Villa's return reached anyone in Mexico, another startling drama took place in the Atlantic Ocean, dominating the headlines in newspapers around the world. The White Star Line's newest cruise ship, touted as the most luxurious and safest vessel to ever sail, hit an iceberg on its maiden voyage from Southampton, England, bound for New York. Just the sort of ship that Lord Cowdray would have loved, the *Titanic* sank on April 14, 1912, and fifteen hundred passengers died in the icy waters. Around the globe, the employees of S. Pearson and Son heaved a collective sigh of relief; their boss had delayed his journey and was not part of the tragedy.

Less than a year after Madero's assumption of power, he was "arrested"
in Mexico City and murdered. The world was horrified; an enraged
Pancho Villa recharged his revolutionary forces, and violence escalated
throughout the country. (Photo source: Family collection.)

A few months later, as El Aguila Oil Company began construction of
a major refinery at Tampico, John Body confided to Lord Cowdray that
he needed someone very special to help him with both the engineering
plans and the supervision of the outlying oil camps. Huge challenges,
including a revolution, were impacting the company's commitment to
deliver on its promise to Standard Oil, and Body told his employer that
he had just the right man for the job.

Samuel William Craigie was a forty-six-year-old widower from England, working for the El Aguila Oil Company, when McNab introduced him to his sister-in-law, Josefina. (Photo source: Family collection.)

Josefina Nivon was thirty-one years old when she married in Salina Cruz in 1914; her marriage certificate lists her as a "spinster." (Photo source: Family collection.)

In Oaxaca, the McNab family had just welcomed another daughter to the tumultuous world of Mexico. Born on April 19, 1914, Easton was named in honor of her Scottish great-grandmother, but Fiona quickly nicknamed her "Baby," an endearment that the family would use forever. Body traveled to Salina Cruz with gifts for the infant and a request that John George McNab become the chief engineer of field construction for the El Aguila Oil Company in Tampico.

Now a family of six, they would travel to Tampico with several loyal servants, household furnishings that included a grand piano, a dog, and a small yellow canary that would most certainly find the long railroad trip difficult. John George frowned at the thought of the journey ahead, but his worries were swept away as his oldest daughters took turns holding their baby sister, cooing with delight. Although his children sometimes perceived him as remote and focused on business, at this moment he was totally present, recognizing a precious moment.

McNab had learned that a marine engineer from England named Samuel William Craigie had been doing a great job in the Pearson oil fields near San Gregorio in Veracruz and that the two men would soon be working together on Mexico's eastern coast. He was a widower, and McNab introduced him to Guadalupe's older sister Josefina, who was thirty-one years old and still unmarried, living in Salina Cruz. The couple married in 1914, another cause for celebration that year.

But there was also sad news. John Body shared the contents of a telegram he had received from Pearson's London offices. Lord Cowdray's youngest son, Geoffrey, had been killed in the new war that was raging in Europe. McNab had been following the conflict through the newspapers of the day.

In June 1914, not long after McNab's annual birthday celebration, Archduke Franz Ferdinand had been assassinated in Austria, and the last few months had seen countries that included Great Britain, France, and Germany take up arms. And now young Geoffrey Pearson was dead, shot during the Battle of the Marne while riding his motorcycle to deliver military dispatches to the troops. McNab sat down at his desk

Guadalupe Fuentes Nivon McNab, circa 1914, confided in diaries
that she feared for her husband's life as he traversed the country,
dodging revolutionaries, and that she wondered what the future held
for her young children. (Photo source: Family collection.)

in the library, took out his finest stationery and pen, and began a note
to Lord and Lady Cowdray. Again, he glanced at the happy scene just
outside the window, where Helena, Estella, Fiona, and "Baby" Easton
played near their beautiful mother. He smiled and sighed and started
to write.

"*As children, we were not allowed in the kitchen, where Petronilla cooked barefoot because she liked the feel of the cool tile floors. Mama always chided her and made her put her shoes back on, but whenever Mama was out of sight, she took them off again.*"

Easton McNab Crawford
Daughter of Guadalupe and John George McNab

Chapter 7

Precarious Times

Tampico: 1915

It was at Tampico that Americus Vespucius, the Italian navigator, first landed on the North American continent. The same harbor attracted the Spaniards in 1497, as they cruised around the Gulf of Mexico looking for new worlds to conquer. Built on a rocky bluff that is forty feet high, surrounded by saltwater lagoons, the region became legendary for its diversity of fish and wild game as early as the 1500s.

By the early 1900s, the architecture of the port city was more American than Mexican, owing to its interaction with New Orleans and other northern ports. The houses were built of wood and stone, with sloping roofs and verandas; they were painted bright shades of blue and yellow, and those surrounding the shaded plaza were especially beautiful. Just outside of town, thousands of orchids grew wild, fed by the tropical sun and perpetual moisture of the region.

In 1915, Pearson put John George McNab in charge of field operations for El Aguila/Eagle Oil in Tampico. (Photo source: Family collection.)

When the McNab family arrived in Tampico in 1915, they were enchanted by the city's ancient church, with wood-carving and frescoes by Spanish artists, and by the colorful marketplace, where Indians sat on palm mats under huge umbrellas selling chiles, jugs of honey, fans and beads, birds and onions, artistically carved wooden implements for household use, and the ever-present marigolds, a flower that was said to bring prosperity and good luck.

The burgeoning oil industry transformed the city of Tampico into a center of sophistication; its plaza was lit by new electric lanterns. (Photo source: Family collection.)

McNab's important new position at El Aguila Oil Company assured him continued prosperity that included a beautiful yellow house right on the plaza, but with the challenges ahead, he knew he could use some good luck as well. Not far from the very best shops, where sophisticated merchandise arrived regularly via steamer from New York, Mobile, New Orleans, Havana, and European ports, the house was in sharp contrast to their recent desert home in Chihuahua. Guadalupe loved the vivid amaryllis and blossoming orchids that clung to the exterior walls of the house, and Helena, Estella, and Fiona delighted in watching the activities in the plaza from their spacious balconies. Each morning they watched as the nanny pushed baby Easton past the central fountain, and at night the plaza was lit with new electric street lamps that transformed it into a place for music and promenades. Young men slowly moved clockwise and *señoritas*, accompanied by their chaperone *dueñas*, moved in the opposite direction, occasionally exchanging secret notes with each other.

From its earliest days, Tampico had modern conveniences for handling cargo, making the port extremely successful; navigable rivers, good land transportation, a working railroad, good climate, and inexpensive labor made it one of Mexico's most profitable agricultural regions. But the discovery of oil, and the development of that industry, was transforming Tampico into a booming center of sophistication, and the McNabs settled into their new life with their usual zest for new adventure.

The *Compañía Eléctrica de Luz, Fuerza y Tracción* had built a new electric tram system in 1914, and wonderful "halfside" cars offered passengers the safety of a vestibule combined with large side windows for ventilation and viewing. John George and Guadalupe often took their four children and the nanny to their nearby beach house at La Barra via the tramway. The ten-mile journey through the fast-growing city was especially exciting in June, when the sea turtles made their annual migration to lay their eggs on the beach.

During the same month, the annual Feast of St. John was another very special occasion for the McNab family. In honor of John George's birthday and saint day on June 24, Guadalupe organized a celebration that became legendary in every place the family lived. Supervising her cook and maids as they prepared chicken tamales with raisins and *mole*, wrapped in banana leaves from the garden, Guadalupe exuded a mix of feminine grace and independent strength. Always dignified and in command of her household, she sat at one end of the long dining room table, resembling a beautiful queen to her young daughters. Her long

A family photograph in Tampico captures John George's pride in his beautiful daughters and wife: from left, Helena, Fiona, Guadalupe, and Estella, circa 1915. (Photo source: Family collection.)

dark hair was braided and coiled into a crown on her head, and when she rang the tiny dinner bell for service, it was impeccably delivered. She deferred to her husband, who sat at the other end of the table, elegantly dressed, with his immaculate mustache and sandy brown hair perfectly barbered.

Guadalupe urged her husband to share some of the history of the feast day with the children, sure that his knowledge of its past in Europe would fascinate both the children and invited guests. McNab explained that by the Middle Ages and Renaissance in Europe, St. John's Day was so important that even the dew that appeared on the grass that morning was believed to have extraordinary healing properties. He told them that precisely at sunset on June 23, St. John's Eve, all men named John set chains of midsummer bonfires along the crests of hills all across Europe, to bless the next fall's harvest. When pressed for more information, McNab pointed to his well-stocked library, with volumes by Chaucer, Tennyson, Keats, and others, and urged them to explore the stories through his massive book collection.

John George McNab celebrated his birthday on the Feast Day of Saint
John, when festive processions moved from the cathedral into the plaza,
and Guadalupe entertained family and friends with games, music,
and native dishes. (Photo courtesy of George O. Jackson Jr.)

In Mexico, the feast day was celebrated differently. Traditional
processions began and ended at the village cathedrals, with faithful
pilgrims and indigenous dancers walking together to honor their patron
saint and to thank him for their answered prayers.

On his saint's day in 1915, John George McNab offered a silent
prayer as he looked down the elaborately set table. Despite the happiness
of the day, and his pride in his beautiful wife and four accomplished
daughters, McNab was preoccupied with the turbulence in the oil
fields, and throughout his adopted country, and was concerned about
his family's safety and future in Mexico; he prayed that rumors of new
unity might prove true. He also was aware that almost exactly one
year before, a war had begun in Europe; and now it was described as a
world war, although neither Mexico nor the United States had joined
the conflict. McNab hoped they would not, recognizing that there was
enough conflict to go around within Mexico itself.

The previous year, forces in the north led by Pancho Villa and Venustiano Carranza, and by Alvaro Obregón and Plutarco Calles in Sonora, had refused to recognize Huerta's government, and a new Plan of Guadalupe had been formulated by them. With an ironic chuckle to himself, McNab wished that *his* Guadalupe had designed the platform, knowing it would have been as practical and well-orchestrated as the feast day coordination and everything else she supervised in their life together.

Named the Plan of Guadalupe to take advantage of the reverence Mexicans felt for their patron saint, it designated the military forces as the "Constitutionalist Army," with Carranza as "First Chief in Charge of the Executive Power," and it promised that upon the occupation of the capital by the Constitutionalists, Carranza would become the interim president and would call for a general election as soon as possible.

All foreign oil operators in Mexico feared Carranza's promise to "restore the oil to the Nation." (Photo source: Bettmann/Corbis.)

The Plan of Guadalupe had gained some momentum in the United States when Woodrow Wilson succeeded Taft as president. Wilson had been shocked at the murders of Madero and Suárez, and at the way that Huerta had assumed power. He determinedly refused to recognize Huerta and made it clear that he would never do so. Huerta would have to relinquish his position before the United States would consider the recognition of any regime in Mexico. The horror stories and gruesome photographs that were being published abroad validated Wilson's stance; it was a true "Mexican standoff."

After just ten weeks, General Huerta's short regime was over; but the violence was not. (Photo source: Family collection.)

Eduardo Iturbide, once part of Mexico's "royalty" and an enemy of the revolutionary government, left Mexico in December 1914, eventually journeying to Washington, DC, where he shared details of his frightening escape in dramatic details with the US secretary of state, and eventually with President Wilson.

A nine-page letter describes his monthlong ordeal of fear—hiding from Pancho Villa's henchmen, jumping from a train to avoid capture, sleeping in the open brush country of Chihuahua with frigid temperatures and howling coyotes, and finally stumbling upon the ranch house of General W. D. Snyman, an English subject who went to Mexico after the Boer War and who helped Iturbide complete his escape to the United States.

Iturbide swam across the Rio Grande, arriving in Presidio, Texas, only to learn that fifteen armed men had just crossed the border looking for him. Two American officials whisked him by car to Marfa, where he boarded a train for El Paso. But that city proved full of Villa supporters, and his guides warned him that he would be assassinated there if he did not keep traveling. He pushed farther west, to Chamberino, New Mexico, where he collapsed with exhaustion and cholera upon arriving at the home of General Snyman's son-in-law.

After his recovery, Iturbide was invited to Washington to share his experiences with government officials, who were struggling to understand the ever-changing situation in Mexico. After State Department official Robert Lansing arranged for him to meet the secretary of war, Lindley Garrison, Iturbide wrote:

> "We talked for two hours; I told him everything I had in me with the greatest of frankness, and discussed energetically his false opinions regarding our situation; and I made him weep with me. He swore that he would save my country and told me I was the man he was looking for a long time. Therefore I hope a great deal …"

Putting action behind his secretary's words, President Wilson lifted the embargo on exports of weapons and munitions from the United States to allow the Constitutionalists to arm and equip themselves, and Huerta's hold began to weaken, although he still had recognition from Great Britain, Germany, and other European powers. In spite of diplomatic pressure and strong representations from people with financial interests in Mexico, including the Rockefellers, Dohenys, and Sir Weetman Pearson,

President Wilson remained adamant—he would not recognize a regime that came into power by revolution and murder.

By spring, after successful fighting in the north, the Constitutionalist Army began moving toward Tampico. The city was an especially critical point for a number of reasons. Its capture would have given the revolutionists a seaport, which they needed badly. It was an oil center of world importance, with refineries, immense oil storage tanks, and producing oil fields clustered together. Large numbers of Americans and other foreigners were employed there as managers and skilled technicians, while most Mexicans there were working as laborers, a condition that aroused deep resentment among Mexicans.

As the army moved south, the United States assembled a strong naval force at Tampico, supplemented by naval support from several other countries concerned for the safety of the city's large population of foreigners. It also sent a strong force to Veracruz, where the German ship that had once taken Porfirio Díaz to safety was now bringing European arms and munitions to the Huerta forces. As intense anti-American feelings grew across Mexico, John Body recommended to his team that both the Mexican and British flags should be flown on all the Pearson company offices in the country.

Although Huerta's coup was quickly ended, the violence continued. (Photo source: Family collection.)

In November 1914, the United States naval forces left Vera Cruz, ending its occupation of the seaport, and just ten weeks later, Huerta's regime ended. But any elusive hope of peace for Mexico was dashed when Carranza and Villa openly broke their uneasy alliance, each striving for power. Various rebel chiefs in the field joined either Carranza or Villa, and the violence escalated.

As the year ended, Francisco "Pancho" Villa had a new ally in Emiliano Zapata, the perennial rebel of Morelos, and on December 6 they triumphantly entered Mexico City. As the "bandit" armies approached, the people of the city—especially the Americans and other foreigners—were terror-stricken. But instead of the expected looting and murder, by some reports the troops were disciplined and respectful. News from Mexico City described Zapata's men as courteous and almost unobtrusive, and Villa's men as impressive in their trademark *sombreros* trimmed in silver and gold. An American woman living there wrote about seeing Villa ride into town at the head of his column, "a stern-faced heavy bodied man, dressed in an elaborate suit of dark blue and gold, hardly recognizable as the Villa I had seen on the border a few years before."

The McNabs also remembered the shabby bandit general who had held little Fiona in his arms in Chihuahua just five years ago, and the fear they had felt on that hot day at the ranch house in the desert. Villa's handwritten note was locked away with other important papers in McNab's library, and when they read the reports of his entry into Mexico City, they marveled at his physical transformation, doubting the stories of an orderly transition, wondering how the ever-escalating drama would play out for Mexico and the McNab family.

Meanwhile, Carranza set up his own government in Veracruz, waiting for the military situation to shift back into his favor. The Carranistas dominated the outlet to the gulf, the entire southeast, and a good part of Tamaulipas, while the rest of the country was controlled by Villa and Zapata. From the announcement of the first reforms at the beginning of 1915 until the oath to the new Constitution in Querétaro in 1917,

When Pancho Villa and his army marched south to Mexico City, accompanied by his new ally Emiliano Zapata, the McNabs remembered their own personal encounter with the famous "bandit general." (Photo source: Bettmann/Corbis.)

Carranza's preconstitutional government would face problems even more complicated than the recent military campaigns, problems rooted deep in Mexican life and history. Land issues, inequalities between rich and poor, the question of sovereignty over natural resources, relations between church and state, and the structure of political power were the dragons that Mexico's next leader would have to confront.

Of deepest importance to Carranza was finding new ways to defend or reclaim the natural resources of Mexico. Determined not to return to the Porfirian tendency of free and easy concessions to foreign investments, especially in oil and mining, he issued a decree in early 1915 that suspended all oil exploitation until a regulatory law could be issued.

The British government quickly recognized the far-reaching, negative implications of this development. In a confidential memo to Lord Cowdray, Foreign Secretary Sir Earl Grey offered help. He suggested that he could instruct the consul at Veracruz to tell General Carranza that the Pearson Company was planning to stop all operations and cancel all contracts with the Mexican Admiralty, forcing it to obtain their requirements elsewhere. Lord Cowdray relayed the offer to his team in Mexico. As always, John Body handled the information carefully, sharing it only with Enrique Creel, John George McNab, and a few other trusted troubleshooters at El Aguila Oil Company. If the Pearson Company played this card, he knew the stakes became more dangerous; on the other hand, surely Carranza understood his country's need for Pearson's expertise on numerous projects under way.

General Manuel Peláez had protected the Pearson oil interests for years; McNab and Body hoped he could continue to do so as the violence in his region increased. (Photo source: Family collection.)

Meanwhile, Carranza assigned Pascual Rouaix, an advisor and engineer, to begin work on a law that would require "the restoration to the Nation of what belongs to it, the wealth of the subsoil, the coal, the oil." In May, Carranza sent Rouaix to observe the operations of the two leading foreign oil companies—El Aguila, Lord Cowdray's British-based enterprise, and Mexican Petroleum, which belonged to the

American magnate Edward Doheny. McNab knew that the refineries, fields, and laboratories of both companies were being closely scrutinized and that Carranza was looking for ways to create a national Mexican petroleum industry.

He hoped that the arrangement that El Aguila had established with General Manuel Peláez, the powerful "feudal lord" of the Huastecan region where the companies operated, would hold. The general was charging $15,000 a month to protect the oil companies against interference from the central government; McNab was uncertain how much longer this strategy would be successful, as Carranza began to take his message to the general public, emphasizing that regaining control of the subsoil was for the good of the nation.

The first half of 1915 witnessed increased fighting between Villa, Carranza, and Obregón, and in June, just days before the McNabs celebrated the Feast of St. John, President Wilson suggested a new "solution to the Mexico problem." He appealed directly to the Mexican people, over the heads of the party and faction leaders, promising that the United States would "give its moral support to some man or group of men, if such may be found, who can rally the suffering people of Mexico to their support in an effort to return to the constitution of the Republic …I feel it to be my duty to tell them [i.e., the faction leaders] that, if they cannot accommodate their differences and unite for this great purpose within a very short time, this Government will be constrained to decide what means should be employed by the United States in order to help Mexico save herself and serve her people."

McNab wondered how President Wilson's thinly veiled threat of intervention would be received by Villa and Carranza, and his worried frown revealed that his thoughts were elsewhere. Guadalupe knew just what to do. She rang her delicate silver table bell for dessert and stepped into the adjoining library.

A smile lit McNab's face when the first notes from Guadalupe's grand piano broke into his somber thoughts, and it grew even larger as Estella added accompaniment on her violin and Helena joined her mother at the piano. As everyone sang the familiar Mexican birthday song "*Las Mañanitas,*" Fiona and Easton clapped happily, and when *pan dulce* and hot *chocolate* were served, the joy was complete.

For the rest of the summer, John George and Guadalupe often remembered that special June celebration. They tried to plan carefree days at the beach, watching the famous sea turtles with the children, but their hearts were heavy as they quietly made plans that would profoundly change the life they knew.

Keeping their deep worries about their children's safety to themselves, they formulated a plan of escape for Helena, Estella, and Fiona; only baby Easton would stay in Mexico. The two oldest girls would go to a prestigious Texas boarding school in the fall, and John George would take Fiona to Illinois to live with his parents. They never revealed their sadness to their daughters; instead, they described the changes as "great adventures" and "opportunities." But sometimes, after the children were asleep, Guadalupe softly played her piano. She let the sad notes express her feelings, capturing the loneliness that she knew would permeate the house once Helena, Estella, and Fiona weren't there. John George read in his library, also haunted by the knowledge that the house would soon be vastly different.

Other families, all over Mexico, were making similar decisions as they followed developments that impacted their world, and the larger drama even extended to foreign soil. When Porfirio Díaz died in Paris in July, some reports claimed he had called out for his lifelong friend, Juana Cata, as he lay dying. And just three months later, she died in Orizaba, en route to Mexico City, still actively involved in politics and trade at age 78.

A special railroad car, arranged by the Mexican government, brought her body to Tehuantepec, where she was buried with all the respect and style one would expect for the wealthiest person in the isthmus. Despite her close relationship with Díaz, she was much admired, even revered, in Oaxaca, and that state mourned the passing of a woman who had risen from poverty and contributed most of her vast fortune to improving the lives of others.

John George McNab sighed; he had admired the entrepreneurial Romero and was appreciative of all that she had done to build schools, restore cathedrals, and empower young women in Oaxaca. He hoped his own young daughters would find empowerment, and safety, in the United States. Meanwhile, he could only wait, and watch the anguished twists and turns of the country he loved, wondering how the tragic dance would end.

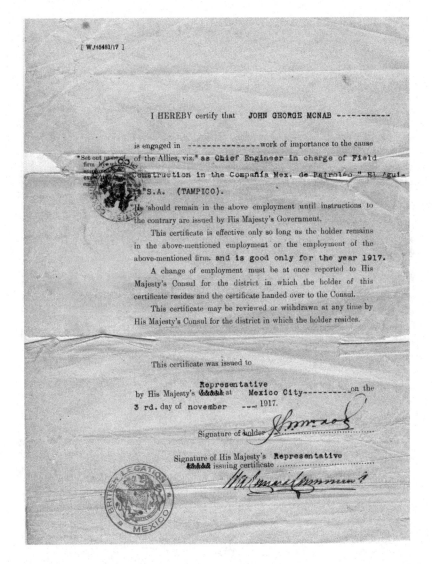

[WJ#5481/17]

I HEREBY certify that   JOHN GEORGE MCNAB -----------

is engaged in --------------work of importance to the cause
of the Allies, viz.* as **Chief Engineer in charge of Field Construction in the Compañía Mex. de Petroleo " El Agui-la".S.A. (TAMPICO).**

He should remain in the above employment until instructions to the contrary are issued by His Majesty's Government.

This certificate is effective only so long as the holder remains in the above-mentioned employment or the employment of the above-mentioned firm. **and is good only for the year 1917.**

A change of employment must be at once reported to His Majesty's Consul for the district in which the holder of this certificate resides and the certificate handed over to the Consul.

This certificate may be reviewed or withdrawn at any time by His Majesty's Consul for the district in which the holder resides.

This certificate was issued to

Representative
by His Majesty's ~~Consul~~ at   **Mexico City**----------on the
3 rd. day of november ---- 1917.

Signature of holder

Signature of His Majesty's **Representative** ~~Consul~~ issuing certificate

"When I was around four years old, my parents sent me to live with my granparents while they explored the art world of New York City. I adored my grandmother—she was so beautiful with her hair in a coil that reminded me of a crown. She was so kind and gentle, but she also had a very strong will. She was the queen of my heart, and when it was time to return to my parents, I didn't want to leave."

Helen Patricia Patteson Cooper
Granddaughter of Guadalupe and John George McNab

Chapter 8

Chaos and Courage

Mexico: 1916–18

Despite Tampico's hot sun, a light harbor breeze lifted the ladies' hats and provided a welcome cooling effect on the crowd gathered on the dock. Guadalupe, Helena, and Estella grabbed their hat brims and smoothed their hair, while five-year-old Fiona laughed as waves of her red hair whipped around her face. Other travelers and sailors stared in wonder at the scene, and as her parents looked on they remembered how, when just an infant, she had produced the same effect on Pancho Villa.

Baby Easton snuggled in the comfortable arms of Petronilla, the almost pure Zapotec woman who had worked for the McNab family since their marriage in Oaxaca. Today she was wearing shoes for the voyage to Texas, something she disliked intensely, preferring always to feel her bare feet on the cool tile floors of the various haciendas. Guadalupe smiled encouragement at Petronilla, and then turned her attention to her elegant husband. John George was dressed, as usual, in a formal three-piece suit, with several newspapers and the latest confidential correspondence between Lord Cowdray and John Body tucked carefully in his carrying case.

Boarding the British steamship *Antilian*, the McNabs traveled across the Gulf of Mexico to Galveston, Texas, just over four hundred miles away from the Mexican port. Still recovering from the hurricane of 1915, the city was undergoing repairs; McNab studied the equipment and construction progress with interest, hoping that the improvements to the seawall would prove strong enough to withstand any new storms that would surely challenge the city in the years to come.

His two oldest daughters would enroll at the Sacred Heart Academy that week, and he hoped that even with its frequent battles with Mother Nature, Galveston would prove safer than Mexico for his little girls.

The Galveston hurricane of 1915 wreaked havoc on the Texas port, with winds that exceeded 135 miles an hour. Helena and Estella McNab matriculated at Sacred Heart Academy just a year later. (Photo source: Galveston 1915 Hurricane Photographs, 1915, Courtesy of Special Collections, University of Houston Libraries.)

The Galveston hurricane of 1915 was a Category 4 storm, with 135 mile-per-hour winds and twenty-one-foot waves. Despite the new seawall, which had been built a few years earlier, the three-hundred-foot beach was hard-hit, becoming an offshore sandbar, and an estimated four hundred people died. Two schooners had been lost in the Gulf of Mexico, and total storm damage was estimated at $56 million, which would be approximately $70 billion in twenty-first century figures.

But the storm had been far less devastating than the infamous Galveston hurricane of 1900, which left six thousand people dead and caused major destruction, including damage to the historic Galvez

Hotel, where the McNabs were staying, and to Sacred Heart Academy where Helena and Estella would soon be boarders.

Founded in 1882 by the Dominican Sisters, Sacred Heart Academy had expanded from its original small building, and now was three stories tall, complete with classrooms for academics, music, and art, dormitories, a chapel, and separate accommodations for the novices and nuns. Its history was well known, beginning with the dramatic train journey of twenty Dominican Sisters who traveled from Ohio to Texas to found the school after their convent and school in Columbus suffered financial problems. Because Galveston was an important port, and the seat of the diocese, Bishop Gallagher had urged them to make the arduous journey and start again in Texas, and they had heeded the call.

By the 1900s, Sacred Heart Academy was one of the most respected learning centers in the region. (Photo source: Archival Collection, Dominican Sisters of Houston, Houston, Texas.)

The trip was difficult, and one of the nun's diaries describes the yellow fever scare that required them to detour on their way to New Orleans. They traveled lightly, with just a clothes basket and a food hamper, and "at regular times we had our meals, said our prayers, and kept profound silence."

Upon arriving in New Orleans, the sisters took another train to the banks of the Mississippi River, which they crossed by boat at Algiers, where they "had a fine view of the big, ugly alligators." They reported that their wool habits made the heat almost unbearable, and at last they arrived in Galveston "thanking God for his many blessings and asking him to continue his love and care in our new home—Texas."

The first school was small; the kitchen had no stove, and water was rationed. When the sisters woke up after their first night in their new home, they had a terrible surprise: "Our faces looked like we had measles—the work of mosquitoes." Here, despite the opposition of the Galvestonians, who did not want "Yankees" teaching their children, the sisters opened their "Select Boarding School and Academy." The Civil War had ended just seventeen years before, and bitterness and distrust of northerners—including nuns—made the first few years difficult ones at the school.

Mother Pauline Gannon was only in her twenties when she became prioress of the school in 1892, and for the next thirty years she was an innovative leader. She insisted that all teachers have college degrees, made improvements to the buildings by adding gardens and areas for physical exercise, and charmed her young students with her intelligence, nurturing spirit, and glorious singing in the chapel. By the mid-1900s, Sacred Heart Academy was one of the most prestigious and respected learning centers in the region.

When the McNab girls were enrolled, Helena was ten years old, and Estella was nine. It was customary during those times for children to attend boarding school at younger ages, much like the European system still in place today. They missed their parents and little sisters, but their beds were side by side in the girls' dormitory on the second floor, and there were exciting new adventures to be had.

Estella had brought her violin and continued her music lessons, and Helena loved the big piano in the school's music room and soon discovered that she had promise as a budding painter. With a total enrollment of nearly 120 students, there were other boarders their age, and the three-story academy reflected serious learning and religious training, as well as its share of laughter and childhood fun.

As a toddler in Illinois, Fiona established a close bond with her maiden aunt, Isabel. (Photo source: Family collection.)

Once school started in the early fall of 1916, Guadalupe stayed in Galveston with little Easton and Petronilla, helping Helena and Estella get settled. The Hotel Galvez was elegant and offered both outstanding service and security for a woman whose husband was making the second part of the journey. John George traveled on with Fiona, northward by train to Illinois, for a reunion with the senior McNabs in Evanston.

After more than fifteen years in Mexico, he was looking forward to seeing his parents, younger brother Joe, and sisters, Easton, Nell, and Isabel. As the wheels rattled along the tracks, he tucked Fiona into bed in their sleeping car, marveling as always at her fiery red hair, and tried to ignore the pangs of sadness that crept into his thoughts as he neared Illinois, where he would leave her during these desperate times in Mexico. Just two years ago, a terrible smallpox epidemic had broken out in the oil fields just outside of Tampico, and the next year, Fiona had been very sick with influenza. Recognizing that their precious daughter's health was delicate had also convinced John George and Guadalupe that time away from Mexico might be best for their red-haired angel.

The reunion in Illinois was joyful, and Fiona's young cousins welcomed her and quickly made her feel at home. Her father told her that she would attend an excellent school, and, like all the McNabs, she would be brave and keep her chin up. The little girl promised; she put her tiny fingers in her grandfather's much larger hand, and agreed to call him *Papá Grande.* John George started his journey back to Galveston, to join Guadalupe and Easton for their small pilgrimage home to Tampico, where their house would seem terribly empty for a while.

When John George McNab took Fiona to Illinois to live with his parents, the family posed for a rare photo; left to right: John McNab Sr. young Jack Potter (son of Easton), Easton, John George, Helen Elizabeth (Nell), Helen Beattie McNab (seated), Joseph, and Isabel. (Photo source: Family collection.)

At eight o'clock in the morning on November 18, 1916, a much larger "pilgrimage" took place. Interim President Carranza staged one of his characteristic triumphal marches from Mexico City to Querétaro, where the long-awaited Constitutional Convention would begin in December. He left the National Palace on horseback, dressed in dazzling military attire and accompanied by fifty other riders, installed his retinue and began to prepare his speeches for the event that the whole world was watching.

No one was watching more closely than McNab, who understood that the future of the country he loved, the hugely successful El Aguila Oil Company where his engineering and managerial expertise were thriving, and his own growing family would be profoundly affected by its results.

On the other side of the Atlantic, as 1917 began, Lord Cowdray was also dressed in his finest attire. With Lady Cowdray at his side, he wore formal white tie and tails as he prepared to accept one of Britain's highest honors, the title of viscount, at Westminster Abbey. The elevation in his peerage from a baron to a viscount came as recognition by His Majesty's Government for the tremendous positive impact his enterprises continued to have on the British economy, and as an acknowledgment of his World War I efforts, most recently the construction of the Gretna Green munitions factory and the tank assembly plant at Chateauroux, France.

Along with an eerie similarity in the pomp and circumstance of both events, there were important political agendas to consider in both places. In Britain, Prime Minister David Lloyd George requested that Lord Cowdray become the president of the Air Board, recognizing the country's desperate need for an increase in the output of aircraft for the war, and the viscount felt obliged to accept the challenge. In Mexico, General Carranza understood that his anticipated presidency would come with tremendous expectations as well.

After two months of passionate debate at the convention, Mexico's new constitution was proclaimed on February 5, 1917. It called for the return of ownership of the land, waters, and subsoil (minerals and oil) to the Nation of all Mexicans (and their representative, the state). It also declared that all churches would become the property of the nation, refused to recognize the church as a legal entity, forbade religious education, and prohibited public religious rituals outside of churches. It established a stronger executive power and a weaker legislative system, creating a more authoritarian presidential regime than the Díaz dictatorship that first sparked the revolution in 1910.

For revolutionary leaders and intellectuals, 1917 would be remembered as the year of the constitution. For most of the Mexican people, it would go down in history as one of the worst years of the century. The government had an enormous debt of almost 750 million pesos; with no internal or external credit, unemployment was rising; the country was in ruins. Crops went unharvested; railroads had been destroyed; mines closed; banks failed; cities were short of food, water and coal; and epidemics of influenza and typhus spread through the country.

In 1917, the Constitutional Convention that was held in Querétaro actually established a more authoritarian regime than the Díaz dictatorship that had sparked the revolution in 1910. (Photo source: Paul Thompson, The Bridgman Art Library, Getty Images.)

Sensitive political updates, including almost-daily confidential cables from John Body, arrived at the Pearson offices in London, reporting that the situation in Mexico was worsening by the day. Now preserved in the Pearson Archive at the Science Museum Library just outside London in Wroughton, they capture the sense of dread that was spreading through the country, as well as the escalating violence.

Europe was in upheaval as well, with World War I raging and Britain actively fighting the Germans. As president of the Air Board, Lord Cowdray had in just a few months nearly doubled the number of British aircraft, and increased oil production in Mexico was fueling the allied war effort.

Despite the political promises of the convention, poverty and crop failures were realities that catalyzed increased violence throughout Mexico. (Photo source: Family collection.)

On March 2, 1917, John Body received a confidential cable from US Secretary of State Robert Lansing, officially confirming that Germany had proposed an alliance with Mexico in the event that the United States declared war on Germany. Part of the offer included Germany's promise to provide Mexico with the necessary funding to attempt a "reconquering" of the border states it had lost in the Mexican-American War.

When railroads, including the Tehuantepec line, were seized by revolutionaries, Body and McNab feared the oil fields would be next. (Photo source: Family collection.)

This followed months of intrigue that began in January when the British intercepted a telegram that the German foreign minister, Arthur Zimmerman, sent to the German ambassador in Mexico City, proposing the alliance with Mexico. At first, the British did not share the information with the Americans, not wanting to reveal that they had cracked the German code. But in late February they forwarded the famous "Zimmerman Telegram" to President Woodrow Wilson, and a few days later, Lansing telegraphed John Body. In April, Wilson went before a joint session of Congress, and the United States officially declared war on Germany, citing the information in the Zimmerman Telegram and escalated German submarine action as the reasons.

McNab met often with Body for updates on the continuous correspondence between Lord Cowdray, top government leaders in Britain and the United States, and important leaders from the political and business worlds of Mexico. Because of his fluency in Spanish and his family's deep roots in Mexico, McNab was often the Pearson company's representative who met with General Peláez, in secret "safe houses" not far from Tampico, passing along payments the region's strongman received for his protection of the oil fields from both the Germans and the *nacionalistas*. He was careful to keep the details of these dangerous journeys to himself, never sharing information about them with Guadalupe or his daughters.

On April 24, Body cabled Lord Cowdray with more bad news. The Tehauntepec Railroad had been seized, and plans were afoot to seize all British railway property. In addition, Mexican sentiment, especially military, had become intensely pro-German now that the United States had joined the war. Body cabled that he feared "other aggressions will follow."

In May, the *Primer Jefe* became the constitutional president of Mexico, an honor Carranza had long awaited. But the economic panorama he faced could not have been more disastrous, and he was quick to realize that it would not be prudent to put all of the new constitutional articles into effect immediately. But he also knew that some actions would be

Violence in the oil fields foreshadowed even
greater troubles ahead for Mexico's most valuable
natural resource and for the foreign companies
involved. (Photo source: Family collection.)

necessary to demonstrate that the new constitution was more than just words.

By early the next year, the oil fields around Tampico were in turmoil. McNab reported to Body that while General Peláez still had sufficient arms to continue his fight to protect them, procurement of ammunition had become a problem. The Pearson team spent long hours discussing whether it would be best for Peláez to give up, submitting to Carranza. Thomas Hohler, secretary of His Majesty's legation in Mexico City, urged the Pearson group to continue its financial and moral support of the general, noting in a memo that "experience has shown that Peláez is willing and able to protect the fields and to prevent Germans or German agents from approaching them," and warning the oil company that General Acosta, a strong pro-German, was advancing toward the center of the region.

Just a few months later, one of El Aguila's paymasters, a Mexican, was shot in the Peláez's Huasteca District on his way to an assignation much like the ones McNab carried out so often. Careful not to worry Guadalupe with this news, John George suggested a holiday trip to Galveston in December to celebrate her saint's day with a visit to the

Multiple revolutionary factions were active all over Mexico—from
Chihuahua to Morelos to Oaxaca—and the country was described as
one huge rebel encampment. (Photo source: Family collection.)

beautiful cathedral there, and several days of shopping and fine dining,
before traveling back with Helena and Estella to celebrate Christmas
at home.

During those darkest days in Tampico, and throughout the rest
of Mexico, the occasional escapes to happier places for John George,
Guadalupe, and Easton were essential. Visits to Galveston were easy and
frequent; the journey could be made by train or by ship, and lovely hotels
along the elegant strand offered the family a welcome respite from their
troubles at home. The girls were doing well at Sacred Heart Academy,
encouraged by the nuns to study hard with plans to attend a university
like the one in nearby Austin. Visits from their parents and little sister
always meant a few special meals at Galveston's new restaurants, and a
shopping spree if their marks were good. From composition books in
the school's archive, it appears that they always were.

Returning to Tampico after each trip to Texas, John George missed
his oldest daughters. Guadalupe found herself listening for their laughing

When he was not troubleshooting in the oil fields, McNab kept an office in Tampico, in the S. Pearson & Son building, which was a smaller version of the London headquarters. (Photo source: Pearson Archive, Science Museum Library, Swindon, United Kingdom.)

voices in the large empty house, wondering how long it might be before the joyful family celebrations of the past would be restored.

To make matters worse, the rest of Mexico was still a huge rebel encampment. In the mountains of Morelos, Zapata continued his own revolution. Felix Díaz was active in the state of Veracruz, hoping to bring back the era of his uncle Porfirio. In Oaxaca there were *Soberanistas* (partisans of their own sovereignty). In Chihuahua, the now legendary rebel Pancho Villa waged his violent revolution against the Carranza regime.

John George and Guadalupe McNab watched with dismay as twentieth-century Mexico demonstrated to the world that the revolution was far from over. These were uncertain times for everyone who had been successful during the Porfiriata period, including the McNabs and all of their Nivon and Fuentes relatives in distant Oaxaca.

Josefina and Samuel Craigie had returned to Salina Cruz and were living in the McNabs' townhouse with their two-year-old son, Alberto, and new baby Millicent Antelma Gertrudis, named to honor both her English and Mexican roots. As a marine engineer, Craigie had completed his work for El Aguila and was assigned to dredge the port, still an important profit center for Pearson. Guadalupe had enjoyed having her sister's family nearby, but she was delighted that the Salina Cruz house was once again beautifully furnished and occupied by loved ones.

El Aguila (Mexican Eagle Oil) faced tremendous challenges as politicians pushed for nationalization of refineries. (Photo source: Family collection.)

Uncertainty gripped Europe as well. John Body had returned to England earlier in the year and had stayed longer than usual in the London offices. Enrique Creel and McNab were busy balancing politics with the destruction and looting that were common near the oil refineries near Tampico, Tuxpam, and Minatitlán to the south. The company's tankers were also under attack, and McNab dreaded the grim reports that came into his Tampico offices, praying that the company's fleet could withstand the Mexican gunboats. Body had promised to return soon; in the meantime, McNab was immersed in field reports for the projected pipeline system that would link the Tampico and Tuxpam Districts by 1918.

When not focused on the immediate concerns of the El Aguila Oil

Company, he spent long hours in his library, studying his *Financial Times,* which was delivered daily, contemplating what creative actions he might take to ensure his family's continued prosperity and security during such chaotic times. In the evenings after dinner, Guadalupe often played the piano and sang, and sometimes the McNabs played cards, a form of euchre, with fast-paced bidding and counting that temporarily took their minds off the frightening violence of the times.

While regular letters from Helena and Estella, and visits to Galveston, eased the sadness of separation, news of Fiona from the senior McNabs in Illinois was not as frequent, due to distance and poor transportation systems for international mail.

As the family's patriarch, "Papá Grande" McNab epitomized the Scottish traits of integrity, self-discipline, and frugality. His wife, Helen Elizabeth Beattie McNab, was so petite that she needed a footstool to reach things; and Fiona was delighted that she was almost as tall as her grandmother. Staunch Presbyterians, the senior McNabs instilled a strong work ethic in their children and grandchildren—a characteristic that Fiona embraced, took back to Mexico when she returned nearly four years later, and valued all of her life.

Her uncle Joseph was a corporate lawyer; and her aunt Easton had married William Potter, an attorney who founded the Chicago Title Company. Their son, Jack, was older than Fiona, but the two cousins became fast friends. Her other two aunts, Nell and Isabella, were the proverbial "maiden sisters." They lived together and doted on Fiona, often combing and braiding her red hair, and regaling her with stories of famous Scottish beauties that had possessed her same special coloring.

As the Christmas season of 1917 approached, Fiona signed her own name, in the careful penmanship of a seven-year-old, to the card that accompanied the huge box of shortbread that the senior McNabs sent to Mexico every year. She remembered how everyone in her family had considered it quite exotic, and that every New Year's Eve in Tampico, she and her sisters would be allowed to drink ginger ale with this most special holiday treat. Born in December like her mother Guadalupe,

Fiona also marveled at the different—but happy—way her birthday was celebrated in this strange new land of winter, snow, and ice.

The box arrived in sunny Tampico, and it was especially savored that year, a poignant symbol of the strong long-distance bonds that linked the two McNab families. Along with the exciting arrival of the traditional box of shortbreads, Guadalupe and John George told four-year-old Easton that she would soon have another special surprise. Helena and Estella had noticed their mother's new curves, and already knew that a new baby would arrive soon, and they laughed with delight at Easton's excitement. This time, instead of being born at home like all the other children, the new addition to the McNab clan would be born in a modern hospital. As the year ended, the entire family traveled to Galveston to wait for that special "surprise."

"*I was the daredevil in the family, and when I was away at college, I decided to have my hair cut in the new 'bob' of the times. When I went home for the holidays, I appeared at the dinner table, very proud of myself. Papa took one look and said, 'You may be excused.' Years later we laughed and laughed about my escapades.*"

Estella Angela McNab Moore
Daughter of Guadalupe and John George McNab

Chapter 9

Beginnings and Endings

Tampico: 1918–20

During the holidays, the city of Galveston sparkled with hundreds of colorful lights strung across the street corners and along the strand, with a massive display in front of the Galvez Hotel, where the McNabs were celebrating *La Nochebuena*. The girls had been disappointed to miss the *Posadas* in Tampico, nine days of processions and fun the week before Christmas, but the anticipation of a new baby sister or brother quickly shifted their thoughts to the adventure ahead. When they sailed to Texas shortly after their mother's feast day, their father promised them that *los Reyes Magos*, the Three Wise Men, would be able to find them and deliver their presents as they always had, even as far away as Galveston.

Shortly after celebrating Guadalupe's thirty-second birthday in Tampico, the McNabs went to Galveston for the holidays and a special surprise. (Photo source: Family collection.)

On the night of January 5, Helena and Estella carefully put their shoes under their beds and helped Easton do the same. Easton announced that it seemed strange that the kings would visit them in a hotel; the older girls smiled and assured her they would. Mexico's celebration of the Epiphany on January 6 symbolizes the journey of the Wise Men, following the star to Bethlehem with gifts for the baby Jesus. And while precious treasures of gold, frankincense, and myrrh were what the Christ child received, children in Mexico hope to find more exciting presents waiting near their shoes when they wake up. Easton had asked for a special doll, Helena hoped for new paints, and Estella had seen a very special pair of fancy shoes in a shop window. Guadalupe, smiling her remarkable smile, told her daughters that she would receive the very best gift of all … a precious baby.

Hotel Galvez, Galveston, Tex.

(Photo source: George Fuermann "Texas and Houston" Collection, 1836–2001, Courtesy of Special Collections, University of Houston Libraries.)

On the *Día de Reyes* there were squeals of delight at daybreak. Just as their parents had promised, the kings had found the Galvez Hotel, and there were wonderful presents for everyone, far more than their little shoes could hold. Two days later John George took Guadalupe to the modern new clinic, just down the street, and on January 8, 1918, Ian Allan McNab was born.

The little boy had his father's bright blue eyes and the famous McNab cleft in his tiny chin. Guadalupe held him gently and said a soft prayer for his safety, remembering the son she had lost eight years ago. Looking at her beautiful three daughters, her eyes filled with tears as she thought about Fiona in faraway Illinois. John George patted his wife's hand, a rare public display of affection, and, smiling, he reminded her that Fiona was probably making a snowman and most certainly still enjoying the box of presents they had shipped in time for Christmas.

Ian Allan McNab was born in Galveston, Texas, on January 8, 1918. (Photo source: Family collection.)

Once the holidays ended, Helena and Estella returned to Sacred Heart Academy, and as soon as Guadalupe could travel comfortably, the rest of the family returned to Tampico. Ian's nursery was waiting, and Easton felt very important in her new role as big sister. Petronilla was barefoot again, happy to feel her feet on the cool tile floor, wondering as always why people in the north liked to wear shoes. Laughter filled the house, along with music and occasional baby cries from Ian; there was a sense of happy new beginnings as 1918 got under way.

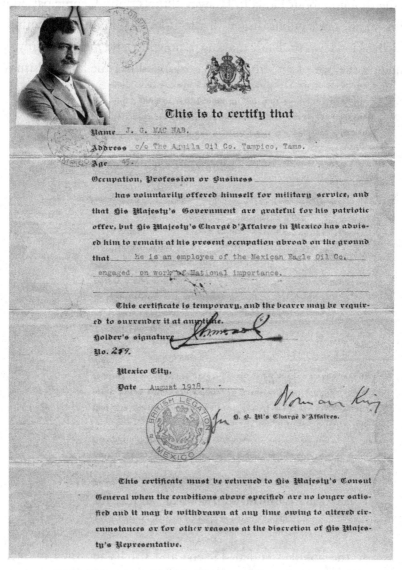

As a British citizen, McNab volunteered for military service during World War I, but his work for Eagle Oil earned him a dispensation. (Photo source: Family collection.)

El Aguila Oil Company's new pipeline had just been completed, and was beginning to transport "black gold" for more than one hundred miles to Tampico. Because of World War I, there was an increased demand for oil internationally, especially in Europe, where multiple battlefronts needed to fuel airplanes, ships, and tanks. Mexico was the second-largest oil-producing country in the world, with an output of more than eighty-five million barrels in 1918, and El Aguila represented more than 60 percent of that production. Pearson's leasehold and freehold properties in Mexico now totaled 1.6 million acres, and more than eight thousand workers were employed in its petroleum enterprise.

International oil operators visited the El Aguila Refinery in Tampico, and the eventual sale of the majority of shares of El Aguila Oil to Royal Dutch Shell was the biggest financial deal in the world in 1919. (Photo source: Pearson Archive, Science Museum Library, Swindon, United Kingdom.)

McNab traveled to Mexico City for more than a week of meetings with John Body, who had recently returned from England. Their conversations were serious and confidential, focusing on the continued efforts of revolutionaries like Emiliano Zapata in Morelos, who was pushing hard for agrarian reform and nationalization of oil deposits, as well as the growing opposition to President Carranza's government. McNab also visited the British legation, volunteering for military service if needed, an expected formality that was quickly rejected. He was issued a certificate from His Majesty's chargé d'affaires in Mexico, noting his country's appreciation and documenting that he was "advised to remain at his present occupation abroad on the ground that he is an employee of the Mexican Eagle Oil Co. engaged on work of National importance."

Tampico's "Golden Lane" produced the majority of Mexico's oil—nearly ninety million barrels by 1919. While the world began to realize the depth and richness of Mexico's deposits, the fields continued to be hotbeds of instability; and Mexican politicians increased their push for nationalization. (Photo source: Family collection.)

Despite the "national importance" that Britain placed on Pearson's Mexican petroleum enterprise, Lord Cowdray had been searching for an exit strategy for at least five years. From the detailed reports from his team in Mexico, and from his own firsthand experiences on countless visits, he clearly understood the situation, recognizing that the new constitution of 1917 would probably mean the nationalization of oil deposits.

He had held discussions with Royal Dutch Shell representatives during the early years of the revolution, and negotiations for a sale by Jersey Standard had been promising in 1916, but the British government, with its military needs at a peak, urgently requested Pearson to discontinue talks. He responded that his company should not be expected to do this, explaining that "the state of affairs in Mexico was such that we should not be justified in continuing to shoulder the whole burden ourselves."

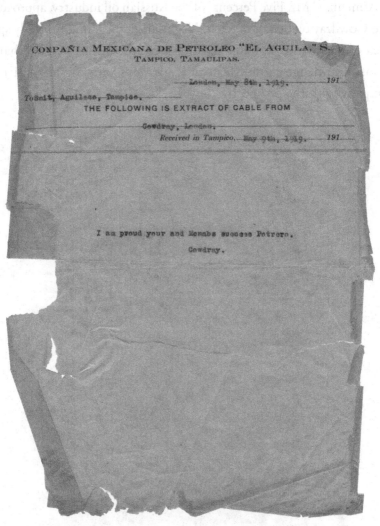

Lord Cowdray praised John Body and John George McNab for their deft handling of his oil enterprise in Mexico, recognizing that they played a major role in moving forward the sale of El Aguila to Royal Dutch Shell in 1919. (Photo source: Family collection.)

Lord Cowdray invited the British government to take a half stake in the business, but its response in 1917 had been to issue new regulations restricting any ownership transfer during the war. In 1918, with the end of the war in sight, the British government removed the restrictions; and Royal Dutch Shell stepped up to the plate.

In October, just a month before the armistice, Calouste Gulbenkian, the Armenian "Mr. Five Percent" of the Russian oil industry, approached Lord Cowdray on behalf of Shell. Negotiations began; John Body spent much of the year in London assisting with the business talks, sharing his vast knowledge about Mexican Eagle Oil Company/El Aguila Oil Company with the prospective buyers.

Roses played an important part in the Miracle of Guadalupe; they were also Guadalupe Nivon McNab's favorite flower. (Traditional prayer card, Oaxaca, Mexico)

McNab remained on the ground in Tampico, overseeing the construction of the huge new refinery just outside of town and thinking about what a potential sale of the oil company might mean in terms of his future. He had worked for the Pearson company for nearly twenty-five years, and as a stockholder in El Aguila, he knew his financial outcome would be excellent. Like Lord Cowdray and Body, he understood the changes that were ahead for the country he loved and considered his own. How would his daughters and baby son fare in the "new" Mexico; what fulfilling work could he undertake in the years ahead?

There were new beginnings to consider—little Ian, the new pipeline and nearly finished refinery, perhaps a move to some new place, and the new experiences that would bring. There were probable endings as well—the world war, his employment with El Aguila, and most likely a departure from the house in Tampico. And, of course, every scenario that danced in McNab's head was set against the changing political landscape of Mexico, the most complicated and beautiful place in the world.

Important visitors from Royal Dutch Shell, and other European oil concerns, came to visit McNab in Tampico, anxious to see the oil camps, pipelines, and refineries in person. Easton, now five years old, often begged to accompany her father on these adventures, and sometimes he surprised her and agreed to take her along. The local workers enjoyed seeing this beautiful child, fluent in Spanish, English, and Zapotec, with dark eyes the color of the oil that was pumped from the ground. They called her *"Chapapote,"* the Spanish word for crude oil or "black gold"; John George shortened the nickname, calling her his little *"Chapa."*

On the other side of the globe, the British naval blockade of all the German ports was having the desired effect. The German people were in dire need of food and supplies; huge protests against the war were taking place in towns across the country, and in late October, the German navy mutinied. By November the "Great War" was officially over, and the allied forces prepared to divide the spoils.

Two of Pearson's three sons returned home safely from their military service, and Lord and Lady Cowdray celebrated at Paddockhurst, the five-thousand-acre estate they had offered to former President Porfirio Díaz after he escaped from Mexico in 1911. Now the winter gardens were at their peak, and enormous greenhouses filled with tropical fruits reminded Lord Cowdray of the warmth and exotic flavors of the country that had made him one of the richest men in England. As 1918 came to a close, the family installed a new clock and bells in the ancient tower on a nearby hill in memory of their youngest son, Geoffrey, who was killed at the Battle of the Marne, in France, in 1914.

Guadalupe McNab shared the same birthday as Mexico's patron saint, and the family never missed the special celebration on December 12. (Photo source: Family collection.)

In Tampico, bell towers were ringing too. The annual celebration of the *Virgen de Guadalupe* began, as always, on the third of December. Nine days of processions and pilgrimages throughout Mexico honored the country's patron saint, leading up to her birthday on December 12. And as always, John George delighted in telling the story behind the tradition. He explained that she was known as the "Mother of Mexico," and was revered for her power, light, and love. Smiling, McNab added that the same was true of his wife, who shared both the saint's name and birthday.

According to legend, in 1531, an Aztec Indian who had been converted to Christianity by the first Spanish missionaries saw a startling vision on a chilly morning in December. A blinding light and unearthly music brought him to a halt as he was crossing a barren hill called Tepeyac to attend Mass. A beautiful woman appeared, surrounded by golden rays that looked like sunlight, which convinced Juan Diego that she was an ambassador from *Huitzilopochtli*, the Aztec sun god, that culture's most precious deity. Her skin color was dark, like his, and she told him she was the mother of Christ, instructing him to tell Bishop Juan de Zumárraga that a church should be built on the hill. The bishop was incredulous when Juan Diego delivered the message; he asked for some sort of sign that might make the story believable. On December 12, the Virgin appeared again and told Juan Diego to pick roses from the dry, barren hillside where no flowers grew, as proof. Miraculously, there were blossoms growing there; the peasant gathered them in his cloak and took them to the bishop. When he let the roses spill out for all to see, a perfect image of *la Virgen Morena* (the Dark Virgin) was revealed, emblazoned on Juan Diego's cloak.

By order of the bishop, a small church was constructed; and a larger one was built in 1709. The Miracle of Guadalupe was officially recognized by the Vatican in 1745, and in 1904 the sanctuary on the hill was declared a basilica. John George explained that now there were churches all over Mexico dedicated to the Virgin of Guadalupe, and that Juan Diego's ancient *tilma* with the emblazoned image of Mexico's

On December 12, festivals and colorful processions took place all over Mexico, honoring the Virgin of Guadalupe, the country's patron saint. (Photo source: George O. Jackson Jr.)

patron saint was still on display in the original basilica. And even in 1918, after 387 years, the image remained vibrant, without any signs of deterioration.

A scholar and historian at heart, McNab had followed the scientific reports about the ongoing analyses of the cloak. He told his daughters that experts had authenticated the fabric as dating to the sixteenth century, but had been unable to determine the type of pigment from which the remarkable image was rendered. Even the ancient dyes produced by Guadalupe's grandfather nearly seventy years ago could not compare with those on the cloak. Then he smiled and asked his daughters to tell him about some of the other mysteries they had been learning about in school, and then clapping his hands for a surprise delivery—a huge birthday bouquet of red roses for their flesh-and-blood mother, Guadalupe McNab.

After nearly twenty years of building up such a large stake in the Mexican oil industry, Lord Cowdray sold 2.5 million shares of Mexican Eagle/El Aguila to the Royal Dutch Company and Shell Oil Company in early 1919. He was sixty-two years old, with great estates in England and Scotland, the father of two sons who were following him in business, and he still controlled organizations with interests and properties all over the world. Royal Dutch Shell paid slightly more than $75 million for the majority of shares in the oil company (about $1 billion in a 2008 economy), and huge profits were realized by the Pearson stockholders. Lord Cowdray continued to own some shares, and formed Whitehall Petroleum Company Ltd. Limited to oversee his remaining oil interests. He reinvested his proceeds from the massive El Aguila sale into his global contracting business, in particular electrical utilities companies in Mexico and Chile, and in a new coal plant in Kent. He ventured into publishing, a new interest that would eventually grow to include *the Financial Times* and the Penguin, Viking, and Simon & Schuster publishing groups. He established various new companies to handle his diverse interests, including S. Pearson and Son Contracting, Whitehall Securities Corporation, Whitehall Petroleum Corporation Ltd., and Whitehall Electric Investments Ltd.; S. Pearson and Son became a holding company.

When Royal Dutch Shell officially took over in April 1919, it was in fact a merger of Britain's largest company with Europe's largest company, consolidating the resulting Shell group's position as the only global rival to Jersey Standard. The British government was one of the largest, if not the largest, stockholders of the Royal Dutch Company; and the sale made international news as one of the largest business transactions that had ever occurred. Oil production in Mexico had grown from 12,546,000 barrels in 1911 to nearly 90,000,000 barrels at the time of the sale, and Pearson controlled 60 percent of it all.

The same month, Lord Cowdray passed his great estate in Sussex to his oldest son, Harold, and he and Lady Cowdray made their Scottish estate in Aberdeenshire their main country home. They had purchased the Dunecht Estate in 1908; it had an immense house and beautiful lochs and woods, and over the years they added the adjoining Forest of Birse, the Raemoir Estate, and the Kirkville Estate to the property, for a total of twenty-eight thousand acres that included some of the best grouse moors in the world. They were renowned for their extraordinary hunting parties and special entertaining that took place in the spring and fall. John Body and his wife were regular guests once they returned to England at the end of 1919, and McNab hoped that someday he would see the extraordinary home he had heard so much about located not far from the castle that had once belonged to his great-grandmother's family.

$75,000,000 OIL DEAL.

Royal Dutch and Shell Companies Buy Mexican Eagle Stock.

The Royal Dutch Company and the Shell Oil Company have purchased 2,500,000 shares of the stock of the Mexican Eagle Oil Company, according to advices from abroad received here yesterday. This is one of the largest oil deals of recent years, the amount involved being approximately $75,000,-000. The Royal Dutch and the Shell Companies will participate in the purchase on the basis of 60 and 40 per cent., respectively.

The Mexican Eagle Company is one of the largest companies operating in Mexico, and is owned by Lord Cowdray. It controls about 800,000 acres of land. The purchase by the Royal Dutch and Shell Companies is said to have been on the basis of $30 a share. Of the total amount of the purchase the Royal Dutch Company paid approximately $45,000,000 and the Shell Company $30,000,000.

The British Government is one of the largest, if not the largest, stockholder of the Royal Dutch Company. It has acquired much of the holdings of Royal Dutch which were held in England, including, it is believed, many shares owned by Germans. Prior to the war Royal Dutch, which is a Holland company, had strong German affiliations.

The New York Times
Published: March 15, 1919
Copyright © The New York Times

The sale of the majority of shares of El Aguila Petroleum to Royal Dutch Shell made headlines around the world as one of the biggest financial deals ever made. (Photo source: Family collection.)

When the Body family decided to leave Mexico in 1919, McNab knew how much he would miss the quiet mentor who had achieved so much for the Pearson Company during his nearly thirty years of residence there. Mostly behind the scenes, out of public view, Body's management style and political shrewdness had brought real success to the company; the vast contracts he supervised in Mexico had easily amounted to more than 11 million pounds sterling. Returning to his home in Surrey, Body continued to office at the Pearson headquarters in London's Westminster district, and agreed to act as a liaison officer between the English and Dutch interests in the Royal Dutch Shell Group. He also joined the board of the old Mexican Railway Company, which was anxious to benefit from his in-depth knowledge of Mexico. During his visits to Mexico over the next few years, Body always planned his schedule to include a reunion with the McNab family; he delighted the five children and Guadalupe with special gifts from London's finest shops, and always brought wonderful tobacco to John George. The two colleagues would reminisce about their adventures on the isthmus, in the northern deserts, and along the coasts of Tamaulipas and Veracruz, recognizing even then that the story they had lived—and were living—was extraordinary.

The Carranza government felt threatened by Emiliano Zapata's work in Morelos, and by his popularity, so it arranged his assassination. (Photo source: Family collection.)

Part of that story took a dramatic turn shortly after the sale of El Aguila, not long after the Bodys had left for England. For years, Body had kept careful track of Emiliano Zapata, a revolutionary general from Morelos, concerned that he posed an especially dangerous threat to the Pearson enterprises. As early as 1911, in confidential memos he named Zapata as an important force to contend with, since he had seceded from the other rebel forces and had organized a band of more than two thousand men as "bandits." His raids and expropriations were highly publicized, and he soon became a heroic figure to Mexican villagers and laborers, much like Robin Hood in England.

Zapata's early criticism of the Madero government for not fulfilling the promises of the revolution and his pressure on the present Carranza government to reclaim Mexican lands had caused serious concern; and after the Carranistas defeated Pancho Villa in late 1917, they managed to isolate Zapata in his home state of Morelos by 1918.

Recuerdo

Little star in the night
That rides the sky like a witch
Where is our chief Zapata
Who was the scourge of the rich?

Little flower of the fields
And valleys of Morelos
If they ask for Zapata
Say he's gone to try on halos.

Little bubbling brook
What did the carnation say to you?
It says that our chief didn't die
That Zapata's on his way to you.

Although Zapata's *Plan de Ayala* was rejected by the various presidents that the revolution had produced, it had been informally incorporated in Morelos, and late that year a US envoy named William Gates traveled to Morelos to observe the results. Upon his return to the United States, he published a series of articles describing the success of Zapata's first agrarian reforms, which included new sugar cooperatives and the first Rural Loan Bank. Impressed, Gates announced that there was "a true social revolution among the *Zapatistas.*" When the articles were read to Zapata, he smiled and said that he could now die in peace.

But his death the following year was not a peaceful one. General Pablo González, in charge of the Carranza government's operations against Zapata, asked Colonel Jesús Guajardo to arrange a secret meeting with the revolutionary, pretending to want to join the agrarian movement. Guajardo obliged, and added another incentive to meet— the promise of a beautiful chestnut stallion named *As de Oros* (Ace of Diamonds).

The son of a horse trader, Zapata could not resist, and when he arrived at the hacienda of Chinameca, he was ambushed and shot to death. Guajardo was elevated to the rank of general and paid fifty-two thousand pesos, and Zapata was elevated to much more heroic proportions. Mexican *corridos* captured the angst of the peasants, who claimed Zapata could never die. Sightings of the famous revolutionary riding his horse in the mountains of Morelos were reported despite the buzzing telegraph lines and newspaper headlines that announced to the world that Emiliano Zapata was dead.

McNab had read with interest the articles about the social revolution in Morelos, published by William Gates in the United States. He remembered stories the Nivon family had told him about the success of agricultural cooperatives in the isthmus during the years that Don Antonio had first made his fortune. And he listened to the popular *corrido* as it made its musical way across Mexico. Beginnings and endings were on his mind.

By fall, the McNabs were considering a move away from Tampico. The transition of the oil operations was going well, and with the profits he had gained from the sale of his own El Aguila shares, there were some

Estella often read to her youngest sister, Easton, and told her stories
about Fiona in far-off Illinois. (Photo source: Family collection.)

interesting investment opportunities in other parts of the country. John
George planned a trip to Mexico City and Guadalajara to investigate
the possibilities, and Guadalupe, Easton, and Ian decided to travel to
Galveston to visit Helena and Estella.

This time the entourage traveled by train, in an elegant private
compartment. Aware that the bathroom facilities, which were down the
train's corridor, might not be conducive to the "potty-training" under
way with Ian, Guadalupe brought along a small chamber pot, as well as
a picnic basket of delicious food and other travel necessities.

Not long into the journey, the train was stopped by bandits. Amidst the sounds of shooting outside the window and general mayhem, Guadalupe quickly hid her toddler under the seat and covered Easton's head with the chamber pot for protection. Although terribly frightening, the assault did not last long, and the bandits rode away on their horses without boarding the train. Shaking with relief, Guadalupe pulled Ian into her arms and attempted to remove the chamber pot from Easton's head. To her dismay, it was stuck. Tears and shrieks followed, until Guadalupe discovered an ingenuous solution. Using her special face cream from a London apothecary shop, she greased her daughter's face and the makeshift helmet was removed.

In future generations, this story would become a McNab family treasure, clearly indicating Guadalupe Nivon McNab's intelligence and courage in the most frightening of circumstances. There would be laughter about the chamber pot stuck on little Easton's head, since everyone escaped unharmed. But as 1919 drew to a close, the beautiful mother of five had nightmares she never shared with her children. She and John George spent long hours in discussion, after the traditional family supper had been enjoyed, after she had played a few happy songs for Easton and Ian, after the nanny had bathed and tucked those precious ones in their beds. They shuddered at the memories of Pancho Villa holding Fiona, of Easton in the oil fields where smallpox had erupted, and of Ian shoved under the seat of a passenger train; but they did not show the unbelievable strain to their children. Instead, they talked about new adventures, perhaps in Mexico City, where pink flamingoes—something Easton and Ian had never seen—wandered in Chapultepec Park, or in Guadalajara, with its fresh air and British compound, which would even make it possible for Fiona to return to Mexico.

"Papa was slow to speak, listened well, and always dressed in a jacket and tie. His favorite spot was his upstairs office, which connected to a small porch above the main porch facing the street. He always sat at his 'Partners Desk' and I would sit across from him and gaze at this gentle and wise man who had such a magnificent and mysterious past. He was a man of habit—his breakfast was always a cup of coffee and a bowl of steaming oatmeal; and at noon, sharp, he had a 'wee bit' of Scotch whiskey before his meal, served in his office."

Laura Helen Moore Brusenhan
Granddaughter of Guadalupe and John George McNab

Chapter 10

Reunion

Guadalajara: 1920–24

Squeals of delight and staccato barks from outdoors turned John George McNab's attention away from the work on his desk in the mahogany-paneled library. He glanced out of the french doors that led to the gardens and smiled. Helena's pet monkey was sitting on top of Ian's head, chattering, and the toddler was laughing as he imitated the funny sound.

Guadalajara, with its thriving British compound, provided a new security to the McNabs, and Guadalupe experienced a more relaxed motherhood with little Ian. (Photo source: Family collection.)

His sisters surrounded him; the dogs—a greyhound and a terrier—were barking, demanding to be part of the hilarity; and Petronilla, barefoot as always, was attempting to remove the monkey. The entire family was together again, and the joy was immense.

Despite his retirement from S. Pearson & Son, McNab continued to travel throughout Mexico for the company, sending updates on the country's political and business developments to the London office. (Photo source: Family collection.)

After a brief stay in Mexico City, where McNab invested in the new Coca-Cola bottling franchise, the family had moved to Guadalajara, joining the large number of British expatriates living there. Their beautiful new house had eight bedrooms and was located on the stylish *Avenida Vallarta*. Its Moorish architectural style and fragrant gardens of jasmine were exotic; and John George and Guadalupe called their new home *La Casa del Alhambra*.

Nine-year-old Fiona had returned from Illinois, and in the fall she and Easton would attend the nearby convent school, *Ecole Française*, until they were old enough to be enrolled at Mrs. Walsh's American School. Helena and Estella would soon graduate from Sacred Heart Academy in Galveston, but their summers were spent in Guadalajara, playing tennis at the British Club and the American Club, and participating in an active social scene of picnics, dinner parties, and costume balls.

Casa del Alhambra was the most luxurious of the McNabs' homes in Mexico, with beautiful gardens, a bedroom for every child, running water, and electricity. (Photo source: Family collection.)

As the June Feast of St. John approached, Guadalupe oversaw the preparations for her husband's special birthday celebration with her usual elegance and organization. With eight servants on her household staff, she was masterful at delegating the chores of cooking, cleaning, laundry and ironing, and gardening. This year, guests would include the British consul and a new circle of friends the McNabs had met in Guadalajara's British compound. Guadalupe had planned several surprises for the party, and the children anticipated that their mother would play a few practical jokes on their father during the week before his birthday.

Conversation at the long, formal table in the dining room was lively, filled with excitement about the first trans-Atlantic radio broadcast and what that would mean in terms of international communication. The discussion turned to the recent assassination of President Carranza and to the June reports published in the *New York Times* about the ongoing investigation. While laughter, music, and delicious *tamales con mole* were being enjoyed inside the Casa del Alhambra on that sunny June day, everyone was aware that Mexico's turmoil still raged just outside the gates.

Venustiano Carranza was dead. His army of Carranistas had been responsible for burning the oil fields near Tampico, and his plans to nationalize Mexico's petroleum business had been a source of worry for everyone on the Pearson team. Nearly six and one-half feet tall, with his long white beard and glasses, he had been a stern leader, and his death had been terrible.

Venustiano Carranza, center, became *Primer Jefe* of Mexico in 1916, and was elected president in 1917. (Photo source: The Bridgman Art Library.)

Born in 1859 to a middle-class ranching family in the state of Coahuila, Carranza was well educated in both Saltillo and Mexico City before serving as mayor of his town, and later as a senator. By 1908, it was assumed that he would become the governor of Coahuila, but President Porfirio Díaz did not confirm him. Bitter about the slight, Carranza supported Francisco Madero in 1910 and became his minister of war when the Díaz government was overthrown.

After General Huerta's coup in 1913 and the assassination of Madero, Carranza united with three other colorful revolutionary generals—Pancho Villa, Emiliano Zapata, and Alvaro Obregón—to depose Huerta. Their alliance was not based on any friendship between them, just the intense shared hatred they felt for Huerta; and when they successfully deposed him in 1914, each general began a separate race for power. Carranza drafted the Plan of Guadalupe and served as the *Primer Jefe* until the Constitutional Convention and his election as president in 1917.

The three years of his presidency had seen more violence and infighting—including the assassination of Zapata, arranged by Carranza's generals—and the isolation of Villa, depicted by the president as a bandit on the run. Obregón had retired to his ranch in Sonora, and in 1919 he decided to run against Carranza for president. He brought his army to Mexico City, where McNab and others around the dinner table had met with the general to hear his plans for Mexico's future, if elected.

In April 1920, one of Obregón's campaign aides attempted to assassinate Carranza. Frightened that a future attempt might be successful, the president decided to flee to Veracruz to regroup and rebuild his political strength. He left Mexico City in mid-May, traveling by train, accompanied by soldiers commanded by General Mariel and a large number of civilians, including the director of the Mexican National Railway.

In a remote part of Puebla, the train was attacked; Carranza and his caravan of about one hundred men were forced to continue their

When the train carrying President Carranza to Veracruz was attacked in the mountains of Puebla, Mexico's leader suspected betrayal, and while hiding in the remote village of Tlaxcalatongo, he was assassinated on May 21, 1920. (Photo source: Anita Brenner, *The Wind that Swept Mexico*, University of Texas Press, Austin, Texas, 1943.)

journey overland by horseback. In the small village of Putla, a local mountain chieftain named Rodolfo Herrera met the caravan and offered to accompany Carranza to Veracruz, with his own soldiers as guards. General Mariel urged the president to accept Herrera's offer, promising to ride ahead quickly, by himself, to arrange for more support in Veracruz. Carranza was worried, and he had every reason to be. On May 21, he was shot to death in the remote village of Tlaxcalatongo, in the state of Puebla.

Over the past month, stories had run in all of the Mexican newspapers, in the *New York Times*, and in publications around the world. Suspicions and accusations had dominated the grim drama, and as John George McNab's guests looked out at the peaceful gardens, protected by the house's massive gates, where the British flag flew at half-staff for the dead president, they spoke in hushed voices about the situation.

According to an article in the *New York Times*, General Obregón had been with a reporter from that publication when the news of Carranza's death arrived in Mexico City. The journalist wrote that Obregón "was deeply moved and immediately ordered the arrest and execution of whomever was responsible, but when later news arrived showing that all of Carranza's aides escaped unwounded, Obregón ordered General Herrera to report immediately to Mexico City."

A few days later, Obregón entrusted the investigation of the incident to four Mexican newspapers—the *Universal, Excelsior, Heraldo,* and *Democrata*—and each of those appointed one reporter to gather information and report. Their findings were published in a May 27 article in the *New York Times*, and the overwhelming consensus was that there had been a conspiracy to assassinate the president.

Indian villagers from Tlaxcalatongo gave firsthand accounts to the *Times*, noting that Carranza had been easily recognized by his height and long white beard, despite the heavy cloak he wore as a disguise. The investigating journalists reported that General Herrera had chosen the "safe hut" for the president and four others (his private secretary, two aides, and the minister of the interior, Manuel Berlanga); and that others in the caravan were placed in other huts in the village, with Herrera's sentinels standing guard. Shortly after everyone was positioned in the huts, Herrera informed Carranza that he had received an urgent message that his brother had been injured. He left the village, promising to return as soon as possible.

At this point in the story, McNab and the other men left the table, retiring to the library for brandy and cigars, wanting to spare the ladies and children from hearing the gruesome finale published in the newspaper. They speculated about Carranza's reaction to Herrera's story about an injured brother, imagining that the president probably knew he was doomed at that point.

According to witnesses' accounts, around three in the morning the hut where Carranza was sleeping was attacked from all sides, with shouts of "Viva Obregón," "Viva Peláez," and "Surrender Carranza" echoing in the stillness of the early morning. Carranza was reported to have shouted that his leg was broken, making it impossible for him to escape; the other four occupants of the hut got away without injury. In the confusion, most of the people in the village fled, and they encountered Herrera about twelve miles down the road.

A "suicide statement" was prepared, claiming that Carranza had taken his own life during the battle. It was dictated by Berlanga, and written by Paulino Fontes, the director of the Mexican National Railway; Herrera took this with him when summoned to Mexico City by General Obregón.

Herrera would no doubt stand trial for the conspiracy, but everyone in the McNab library expected he would be acquitted, and a few months later, the courts would prove them correct. John George thought about his meetings with Obregón over the past few years, and remembered the many times he and John Body had met with General Peláez to discuss his protection of the oil fields during changing political times. He preferred both revolutionary leaders to the Carranza regime, and during the summer months he watched to see who would emerge as the country's next president.

Vice President Adolfo de la Huerta served as provisional president until elections could be held at the end of the year. As expected, General Alvaro Obregón was victorious; he assumed the office on December 1, 1920, becoming the eleventh successor to Porfirio Díaz in just a decade. From the Obregón meetings that had taken place in the beautiful library of the Casa del Alhambra earlier in the year, McNab knew that the president's focus would be on agrarian and anticlerical reforms, and

General Alvaro Obregón was in position to reinvent the war-torn
nation of Mexico after President Carranza's funeral brought an end
to the strong-arm tactics of his administration. (Photo Sources: (left)
Paul Thompson, The Bridgeman Art Library, Getty Images; (right)
The American School, The Bridgeman Art Library, Getty Images)

that he hoped to cultivate better relations with the United States. To
achieve this, he planned to increase the sales of Mexican petroleum to
the US market; this was good news for everyone concerned.

It was a relief to put the day-to-day responsibilities of the oil business
behind him, and McNab was grateful that Royal Dutch Shell would
now be the one dealing with the political roller coaster ride that he
knew all too well. Body had worked out a consulting agreement with
them, and his knowledge of Mexico and its power structure would be
invaluable. McNab also was involved in some related projects, including
the provision of steel storage tanks to various refineries, and the final
months of construction of the large new refinery in Tampico. But for
the most part, he did not scan the daily newspapers with the sense of
dread he had felt over the past few years, worrying about the latest attack
on the railroads or destruction in the oil camps. He felt a slight easing
of the tension he had carried for the past few years, daring to savor the
pleasures of home and family.

Guadalupe was overjoyed when all of her family was reunited in Guadalajara.
Standing, left to right, are Estella, Fiona, and Helena; Guadalupe is seated,
and Ian and Easton are seated at her feet. (Photo source: Family collection.)

Lord Cowdray also felt a new distance from the nightmares of
revolution. In early 1921, he corresponded with several Americans who
were still actively working in the Mexican oil business, and who had
developed a "Five Chapter Plan" to keep the industry viable as Mexico
shaped its political future. As always, John Body lent his expertise to the
effort, and on behalf of the oilmen, shared the details of the plan with
Lord Cowdray. The viscount's response was courteous and appreciative,
but clear that "my attitude is now rather that of an onlooker than a

participant, for the handling of all Mexican political questions in their relation to our oil interests now rests with our friends at St. Helen's Court."

Other interests were occupying John George McNab as well. Excited about the nascent road system under construction in Mexico, he was confident that over the next few years, automobiles would become as important as the railroads for transportation throughout the country. There was talk of building a new Pan-American Highway that would eventually provide an all-land, all-seasonal connection between the United States and the Panama Canal, and, although it was not completed for more than a decade, the early dream was seductive.

Cars were already popular in big cities like Guadalajara, Tampico, Mexico City, and Veracruz; and new models with more powerful engines and fancy body styles were making their appearance on the newly paved roads. With some of the profits he had realized from the sale of his El Aguila stock, McNab bought the Starr Durand Automobile Agency and began importing vehicles from the United States.

John George McNab was confident that Mexico's evolving road system would create new opportunities in the transportation business; he bought an automobile agency and his first car— a Studebaker that could reach speeds of 50 miles per hour. (Photo source: Family collection.)

Arriving at the gates of Casa del Alhambra, he honked the horn of his new Studebaker, smiling at the surprised looks on the faces of Guadalupe and the children as he drove down the long entrance road to the house. The car's white wire wheels and clear Eisenberg windows were state-of-the-art technology, and its large six-cylinder engine could deliver a speed of 50 miles per hour on a paved road.

The Studebaker Brothers Manufacturing Company was established in Indiana in 1852, producing wagons for farmers, miners, and pioneers moving west to the new frontier. It manufactured the immensely popular Conestoga covered wagons, and in 1902 it introduced the first electric car and sold 1,841 of them. In 1912, the company developed the first automobile with a petrol engine, and by 1920, it had abandoned the wagon business and only made cars. In 1922, the company earned $100 million, and its six-cylinder touring cars were the most popular automobiles in the United States.

Ian, Guadalupe, and Helena (standing), circa 1921, in Guadalajara. (Photo source: Family collection.)

As the automobile era began in earnest, other modern advances were changing the world in equally important ways. In the United Kingdom, the British Broadcasting Company began radio service, delivering news and entertainment to its audiences instantaneously. It was possible to hear firsthand accounts of the imprisonment of a small, brown-skinned lawyer named Mahatma Gandhi in India, as well as the election of Calvin Coolidge as president of the United States, and recordings from New Orleans of a young jazz musician named Louis Armstrong echoed through the cities and smaller villages of England. Thanks to amazing new transportation and communication systems, the world was getting smaller.

On rare occasions in the relaxed setting of Casa del Alhambra, Guadalupe would let her long chestnut hair escape from its elaborate, carefully coiled style. (Photo source: Family collection.)

In early 1922, happy news came from Salina Cruz that Guadalupe's sister Josefina had had a third child—a baby boy named Federico in honor of his grandfather. But before the year ended, the little boy died, another victim to the infant mortality rate of the times. Guadalupe and John George remembered their own heartbreak when little John Allan died in Salina Cruz before he reached his first birthday.

The death of their nephew Federico Craigie, in Salina Cruz, reminded Guadalupe and John George McNab of their similar heartbreak in 1910. In those times many children died before their first birthdays; and their brief lives were celebrated as lovingly and elaborately as possible. (Photo source: Family collection.)

The journey from Guadalajara to Galveston still was not easy, and each fall John George and Guadalupe accompanied Helena and Estella back to school at Sacred Heart Academy. The trip entailed taking a Mexican train north to Eagle Pass, first crossing the desert lands of

Sonora and Chihuahua, where Fiona had been born nearly thirteen years ago. The monotonous and desolate landscape provided a bridge to the past, and suddenly McNab was confronting the memory of Pancho Villa, filthy from days on the trail, holding three-month-old Fiona in 1911. Forcing his mind back to the present, he acknowledged an almost psychic connection with the colorful revolutionary who had written a personal letter of safe passage for the McNab family, remembering his triumphant march into Mexico City a few years ago, finely dressed and wearing a sombrero inlaid with silver. Just a few months ago, in July, Villa had been ambushed and killed not far from home, where his pregnant wife was waiting for him. "I am a part of all that I have seen," McNab thought, quoting the poetry of Tennyson with a shudder.

Despite the idyllic security he enjoyed in Guadalajara, McNab realized that violence was still an integral part of life in Mexico, documenting it in photographs he took for the Pearson Company. (Photo source: Family collection.)

Crossing from Mexico into the United States at Eagle Pass, the travelers transferred to the same railroad line that had once given McNab access to a "big city" when he worked on the remote Thomson Ranch. The family would disembark to spend a few days in San Antonio, staying at the elegant Menger Hotel, where Lord Cowdray had written his now-famous cable to John Body more than twenty years ago instructing him to buy land in Mexico.

During the long days of railroad travel, McNab poured over his newspapers, paying special attention to his copy of *the Financial Times*, and he always took along one of his favorite poetry books, usually by Tennyson or Keats.

The 1923 train ride to Galveston was special; it marked the last fall journey to the academy. Helena and Estella would graduate in the spring. A chapter in their life adventure was coming to a close, and a new one would soon begin. John George and Guadalupe already were investigating the best colleges in the area, determined that all five of their children would graduate with degrees from universities.

John George was proud of his two oldest daughters; they had excelled in school and were talented musicians and artists. Helena had produced watercolor paintings during the summer that were of such professional quality that Guadalupe had placed the best ones throughout the Casa del Alhambra.

As he glanced at his two "young ladies," he realized how beautiful they had become. Both dark-haired and dark-eyed like Guadalupe, they were dressed in stylish traveling clothes, wide-brimmed straw hats, and white cotton gloves. He smiled at the memories that came rushing forward—Helena on her first pony in Salina Cruz, Estella nestled in his arms at the Santa Gertrudis ranch—and he spoke softly, quoting Keats, "A thing of beauty is a joy forever; its loveliness increases; it will never pass into nothingness."

As always, the McNab family celebrated Guadalupe's birthday in grand style, knowing that almost everyone in Mexico was doing the same thing, lighting candles and making pilgrimages to honor the country's patron saint. The Christmas holidays were fun-filled and happy, and to end the year, the McNabs entertained their friends at a costume ball at Casa del Alhambra. Guadalupe was well known for her extraordinary parties, and she loved planning events that had themes and special surprises. The British consul general, Percy Holmes, never missed the opportunity to attend these gala affairs. There was always music, dancing, exceptional food, and intelligent conversation about world affairs and the challenges that were closer to home.

Holmes had become a hero in the United States, following his courageous rescue of 245 Americans who were under attack in Guadalajara in 1914. The US Consulate was sacked and looted, and its consul was "marked for death" by Sebastián Carranza, a nephew of the president that Mexico would elect a few years later. As thousands of Mexicans rioted in the streets, protesting the ever-growing presence of Americans in the region, Holmes arranged for a special train to take the 245 captives to Manzanillo, on the Pacific Coast, where a German steamship took them to safety in California.

In 1920, the US Senate began an investigation of "the Mexican situation," hearing testimony from many who witnessed the riots in Guadalajara and the atrocities in other regions. Dr. John Hunter, a physician employed by the American mining companies operating near Guadalajara, described the heroic efforts of Holmes in 1914, as well as some of the other frightening experiences he had endured. The *New York Times* published parts of Hunter's testimony; McNab had read the series carefully, and knew only too well that the descriptions were accurate.

According to the newspaper, Hunter told the members of the Senate that there was "a gruesome practice in Western Mexico, where they hang men not by the neck, but by putting ropes under their arms and suspending them in the air from the limbs of trees. Then their feet are cut off, and the victims are shot." McNab had seen men hanging from the trees; it was part of the nightmare that he tried to keep from Guadalupe and his five children. He had documented the

Fiona, Estella, and Helena (left to right) had been sent away to
school during the worst years of the revolution; in Guadalajara the
family was reunited at last. (Photo source: Family collection.)

violence by taking photographs for the Pearson Company, capturing
terrible scenes he would never forget, despite the relative safety of the
British compound in Guadalajara, and early indications that President
Obregón's administration was an improvement.

Estella McNab was accomplished on the violin, and was
selected to play a solo in the graduation concert at Sacred
Heart Academy. (Photo source: Family collection.)

As 1924 began, the long dormant volcano at Mount Orizaba erupted,
spewing showers of sulphur into the sky. McNab remembered the violent
eruption of Mount Colima at the dawn of the Mexican Revolution, a
foreshadowing of the end of the Porfiriata, and he wondered if this new
upheaval was also an eerie prophecy of change.

Ian McNab spent a carefree childhood at Casa del Alhambra, never imagining the horrors of revolution that his father had seen. (Photo source: Family collection.)

Politics were in the spotlight again, with Adolfo de la Huerta leading a revolt against the Obregón government in a bid to be the next president. But Obregón preferred a general named Plutarco Elías Calles. Still dedicated to important businesses and friends in Mexico, John Body made sure that Calles was entertained in style by Lord Cowdray and other British nobility when the Mexican general visited England during the summer prior to the elections. In November, Obregón stepped down from office when Calles was elected president; new leadership would mean change, again.

The year also brought major changes to the McNab family's personal world. Helena and Estella graduated with honors from Sacred Heart Academy, and the ceremony in Galveston featured both of the graduates on the program—Helena played the piano, and Estella read a winning English composition. Both had been accepted at the University of Texas in Austin, and they would live in the beautiful new dormitory that

Family was all-important to John George, pictured with Estella and Ian, and his favorite greyhound, and as 1924 came to a close, some major "life chapters" ended, making room for new dreams. (Photo source: Family collection.)

Sacred Heart Academy had just built in the state's capital city. Just as this new generation moved toward adulthood and fresh expectations, the older generation lost its matriarch when Helen Elizabeth Beattie McNab died in faraway Illinois.

As John George grieved the death of his mother, Fiona put her small hand in his, feeling a deeper sorrow than the other grandchildren because of the years she had spent with her *Mamá Grande*. The name always made her smile, because her grandmother was certainly not "big" at all; she had been tiny in stature, and Fiona had been delighted when she grew taller than the little lady who tucked her into bed for four years in Evanston. She loved her extended family in the north, and at nearly fourteen years old, she knew that her father's favorite poet was right when he said "love is the only gold."

"In June, for the San Juan feast day, Mama and the cook made special square tamales made out of chicken and raisins, seasoned with mole and wrapped in banana leaves from the tropical garden she grew. Every week the vegetable man would come down the street and Mama bought fresh vegetables from him. She drove a little Studebaker with red leather interior, and she always turned the rearview mirror down so she would not see the cars behind her. That scared me until she explained that she'd learned to always look forward—not back—during the Mexican Revolution."

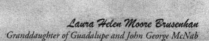

Laura Helen Moore Brusenhan
Granddaughter of Guadalupe and John George McNab

Chapter 11

Revelations

San Antonio, Texas: 1925–60

Leaving the luxuries of Guadalajara was not easy. Still more difficult was the farewell to Mexico, where Guadalupe's roots went back to that country's earliest inhabitants on the isthmus. It was the country that John George had considered home for his entire adult life, and all of his professional and personal accomplishments had occurred there.

At fifty-three years old, John George McNab had lived his entire adult life in Mexico; forty-year-old Guadalupe was still strikingly beautiful and talented, embodying all that he loved about his adopted country. (Photo source: Family collection.)

From the day he arrived in Veracruz in 1896, he had loved the colors and sounds—so different from misty Scotland and the snows of Illinois—and the people who had welcomed him into a new world with a warmth and vibrancy unlike anything he had ever known.

Now fifty-three years old, McNab recognized the blessings of a full life—he had a beautiful, intelligent, and loving wife and five children, and he had experienced adventures that were every bit as exciting as the heroic tales he had read as a little boy in Crieff. His engraved gold watch from the Pearson Company symbolized the twenty-five years he had spent supervising railroads, ports, and oil fields; but the memories of his first dance with Guadalupe, the flowers and fragrances of her garden, the sharp whistle of the trains on the Tehuantepec route, the dark eyes and hair of his first daughters, followed by Fiona's blue eyes and red curls, and Ian's blond locks—even the dangerous encounter with Pancho Villa and the secret meetings near the oil camps—were even more precious, woven together into a rich tapestry of life. He was proud to have played an important role in bringing much-needed infrastructure to the country he loved, and his ongoing friendship with John Body was even more satisfying than the watch he wore with such pride. The nightmare years of President Carranza were over, and the extraordinary security concerns he had felt had diminished. He had known six Mexican presidents during the twenty-eight years he lived in various cities in the states of Oaxaca, Chihuahua, Tamaulipas, Jalisco, and the Federal District. He and Guadalupe had witnessed modern changes— they both drove automobiles, enjoyed electricity and running water in their homes, and owned a radio that kept them informed about the world. And they cherished the ancient traditions that they had discovered in every new place they lived, incorporating them into their annual feast day celebrations and into their children's cultural education.

The Nivon and Fuentes families were scattered throughout the state of Oaxaca, and a few adventuresome cousins had moved to New Orleans. The relatively small number of McNabs in Illinois had just

John George was proud of his daughters, Helena and Estella; they both attended the University of Texas at Austin and had inherited their mother's beauty. (Photo source: Family collection.)

lost their matriarch; and Helena and Estella would soon leave Mexico to make new lives at a university in neighboring Texas.

At the close of 1924, John George McNab decided another bold move was in order. After discussions with Guadalupe, he decided to relocate the family to San Antonio, where the architecture and ambience were similar to those of Mexico. It was a city where he could pursue investments as well as American citizenship. He told his family about it, quoting Tennyson: "Tis not too late to seek a newer world."

San Antonio was not really new to John George; he had spent happy times there as a young man when he worked on the Thomson Ranch near Eagle Pass, and the entire McNab family had enjoyed stopping there for a few days of shopping, dining, and theater whenever they traveled by train from Mexico to Galveston. They purchased a large and beautiful home in the new neighborhood of Monte Vista, just a short trolley-car ride from the older residential areas near downtown.

Located at 618 Russell Street, the house had a private bedroom for each child, a sleeping porch across the back, and several guest rooms, as well as a separate guesthouse and an apartment over the garage. Its front porch framed both stories of the house, and patios on both sides and in the back caught the breezes that brought a bit of relief to hot Texas afternoons in the days before air conditioning. As always, Guadalupe had lush gardens filled with flowers and blooming trees, and John George often took his afternoon *siesta* in a colorful Mexican hammock that he brought with him from Guadalajara, hung between two large trees in the side yard. Chinaberry trees graced the back patio, which also had a fountain and fish pond, and dogs, cats, and songbirds created quite a menagerie outside.

The McNab house was located in the elegant Monte Vista area of San Antonio and was furnished with wonderful treasures that the family had brought from Mexico. (Photo source: Family collection.)

Furnished with beautiful antiques, including the well-traveled grand piano, and some fine pieces from Mexico, the rooms downstairs were elegant and eclectic, graced with some of the more informal influences of the years spent in Oaxaca and Jalisco. The McNabs often entertained friends; meals were always memorable, and the evenings usually ended with a fast-paced card game called Pitch.

Guadalupe McNab (second from left) and her daughters Fiona (far left), Estella, Helena, and Easton kept a menagerie of pets at their Monte Vista home. (Photo source: Family collection.)

Helena and Estella were freshmen at the University of Texas, living in Newman Hall, a residence for women that had been built by the Dominican Sisters in 1918. It was the first residence hall in the country to operate under religious auspices; and it offered a perfect segue from Sacred Heart Academy. Fiona and Easton attended the primary school, Urseline Academy, at Our Lady of the Lake University, and Ian was enrolled at Travis Elementary School, located in the Monte Vista neighborhood.

Top: In 1925 the McNabs sailed for Europe; at last John George could show Guadalupe the Scottish thistles near the family home in Crieff that he had so often described to her. *Bottom*: During their tour of the continent, the McNabs visited Spain to see the original Alhambra. (Photo Sources: Family collection)

McNab maintained an office at Bache & Company, one of the major stock brokerage firms in the country at the time. He worked on his growing portfolio of investments, and in these years of semiretirement began to make sure all of his affairs were in good order. Every day he dressed in coat and tie, sometimes adding a splash of Florida water cologne to his face; and his British pronunciation of the English language added even more elegance and dignity to his persona.

Guadalupe was always deferential to her husband, very much a product of her times, but her quiet strength and opinion were also part of every decision John George made. Recognizing her courage in leaving her homeland to relocate in Texas, he looked for a way to thank her for her constant support and to celebrate their liberation from the political challenges that had been such a part of their lives together.

In the summer of 1925, the couple sailed for Europe, on their first Grand Tour, an extended trip to France, Spain, and the United Kingdom, where they visited the places their ancestors had lived before they embarked for new worlds. They met distant Nivon and McNab relatives, enjoyed the famous Ascot races with the John Bodys, and dined with Lord and Lady Cowdray in London.

In order to be away for several months, the McNabs placed their three youngest children at Sacred Heart Academy in Galveston, where Helena and Estella had completed their earlier education, knowing they would be safe and happy there until their educations were resumed in various schools in San Antonio in the fall.

They sent regular cables, and colorful hand-painted postcards of castles and lakes in Scotland, the new Eiffel Tower in Paris, and the ultramodern "golden lifts" that had made London's Selfridge's department store so famous. When they returned to Texas, they would delight in describing the ride on the gilded elevators to the top floor, where Guadalupe was assisted by prim and proper English salesladies who were astounded by her dark, exotic beauty.

The Pearson offices in London, although larger and grander, had the same architectural design as McNab's office in Tampico. (Pearson Archive, Science Museum Library, Swindon, United Kingdom)

On June 12, John Body and John George McNab met at noon at the Pearson offices on Parliament Street, in the Westminster district of London. The colleagues reminisced about their years working together in Mexico, the difficulties and ultimate rewards associated with the Tehuantepec Railroad and the Salina Cruz port operations, and the multitude of challenges they had faced while running Mexican Eagle Oil. Both men had worked for "the Chief"—as Lord Cowdray was called by his team—without any desire for public recognition or fame, and they had always been extremely cautious about discussing the sensitive diplomacy they carried out so effectively during the Mexican

Revolution. Both had hidden the dangerous side of their work from their wives and families, and their reunion in London provided a very special opportunity to remember adventures that only they knew about.

A week later, Lord Cowdray sent a personal invitation to McNab, delivered by hand to the Imperial Hotel, inviting him to lunch at his private club on June 26. Now one of the wealthiest men in England, the visionary engineer and entrepreneur welcomed his former protégé warmly, asking about his family and congratulating him on his wise decision to invest in his extraordinarily successful new Amerada Oil Company. With a twinkle in his eye, he issued an even more exciting invitation at the end of lunch.

The weekend party at Dunecht House in Aberdeenshire in mid-July was one of the most sought-after invitations in Great Britain, offering several days of hunting, elegant meals, and fascinating company at one of Scotland's most beautiful country estates, hosted by Lord and Lady Cowdray. Nearly seventy years old, and despite failing health, the viscount was renowned for his hospitality and for his love of a good party.

John George and Guadalupe were thrilled to accept, and much like he had "brushed up his best coat" many years ago in Veracruz, before meeting Guadalupe, John George enjoyed selecting some beautifully tailored suits for himself and special hunting attire for his wife in some of London's finest shops. Both were looking forward to meeting Lady Cowdray for the first time. They had heard the Chief extol her virtues over the years; he liked to say that his marriage to her was "the supreme event in his career." John George smiled fondly at his beautiful wife, and knew he felt the same way.

Annie Viscountess Cowdray had been born in Yorkshire, like her husband; she was the daughter of Sir John Cass, a successful industrialist from Bradford. She had married Sir Weetman Pearson in 1881, and their courtship had romantic aspects that were similar to those of John George and Guadalupe.

As a young contractor, Pearson had completed a massive project in Palestine; to celebrate his return, he invited a party of friends to see some of the treasures he had brought back from that ancient land. Among them was a Bible bound in olive wood. During the course of the evening, he announced that it was intended for his future wife; and after the party was over, he offered it to Annie Cass, who was then seventeen years old.

She refused, but Pearson's wooing was marked with the same persistence that took him to the very top of his profession, and he was sure of his choice. A year later he again offered the Bible to Annie, and she accepted. After just a year of marriage, when Lord Cowdray's firm had captured the contract to build a railway in Spain, she went to the project site with him, sharing rough quarters, terrible food, and exposure to bad weather. Afterward the Pearson contractors said that she had "saved their lives by going ahead to see that hot food and dry sheets were waiting for them at the end of their day's ride or march."

Dunecht House in Scotland was the legendary estate of Lord and Lady Cowdray. (Photo source: Ian W. G. Sutherland, Aberdeen, Scotland.)

Now, more than forty years later, everyone was assured of remarkable luxury at the end of the train ride to Aberdeenshire. The very best Scotch whiskey, delicious meals, and comfortable bedrooms were waiting at Dunecht House, and every invited guest treasured the time they would spend with the woman who "shared with head and heart" Lord Cowdray's successes and failures. She was known for her philanthropy, and often described the "delight" she found in giving to women's causes. Her latest project was a new hospital for women, run by women, entirely staffed by women, where medical women could enjoy extended opportunities for training. Queen Mary had voiced support for the project, and as was her custom, she already had paid a visit to Lady Cowdray at Dunecht when she moved her retinue to Balmoral Castle earlier in the summer.

Guadalupe loved the stories about Lady Cowdray, and realized that she had similar traits. And like her hostess, she had married a man who was both forceful and reserved, and she had shared some rough quarters at times during her life with John George in Mexico. While their houses in Salina Cruz, Tampico, and Guadalajara had been elegant and luxurious, the ranch house at Santa Gertrudis and the field houses in Chihuahua and near the Potrero field had not even had running water. As the first-class train traveled through the moors of Scotland's lowlands, Guadalupe saw the thistles growing wild, and she remembered the kneeling pillow she had made for her husband, for their wedding more than twenty years ago. At times he could appear as austere as Scotland's hearty native plant, but she noticed that as he read his book of poetry, his gaze softened, and he reached for her hand.

The journey north from London had been interesting, past the industrial centers of York and Newcastle, to Edinburgh. They traveled through the center of Scotland, taking a side trip to see the Hawkshaw Cottage in Crieff, where John George was born more than half a century ago. The Caledonian Sleeper train offered comfortable private drawing rooms with special berths for overnight travel, and as they continued north past Dundee to Aberdeen in the northeast corner of the country,

John George watched the mauve and lavender hues of heather in the fields and felt a lump in this throat, despite his calm and reserved exterior.

In the heart of his native country, McNab knew the time had come to share an old but important story with his wife. He took her hand, and quoted John Keats, "I am sure of nothing but the holiness of the heart's affections, and the truth of imagination."

Shortly after joining the Pearson Company in Mexico, while working on early plans to build the Tehuantepec Railroad, McNab had met and married a young woman he met in Veracruz. After only a year of marriage, she died in childbirth; and the young father had no idea how he would raise a baby daughter. But McNab's in-laws were young themselves, and they convinced him that they could offer the best life to their tiny granddaughter. They were bound for California, and they promised to love and care for the infant. McNab knew his work with Pearson would require constant travel and often primitive conditions, and he accepted the plan with both sadness and gratitude.

As he told Guadalupe about the daughter he had never known, his wife's eyes misted, and she thought about the mother she had never known. Stories of this kind were not unusual during those years when childbirth often brought death, and there was a practical understanding that those who survived had to continue with their lives as best they could. John George felt relief that he had revealed this ancient secret to the wife who was the recipient of his "heart's affections," at the same time recognizing that he could never share the most horrific moments he had experienced when the oil fields burned and revolutionary hangings were rampant. Those would remain secret until his dying day.

They talked briefly about his plan to provide a small stipend to his daughter upon his death, and Guadalupe fully supported the idea, secure in the fact that she and their own five children would be well-cared for by John George's very comfortable estate, which included real estate, an excellent portfolio of stocks, and other investments. With absolute solidarity, and excitement, they prepared to leave the train, realizing that they were about to see firsthand the vast estate of one of the wealthiest families in the world.

In the mid-1920s, members of the Nivon family often met at the beach north of Salina Cruz, not far from the Santa Gertrudis Ranch. (Photo source: Family collection.)

The long weekend at Dunecht House met all expectations; when the McNabs returned to San Antonio, they captivated their oldest daughters with descriptions of the castle, beautiful guests, gourmet feasts, and evening dances. Ian was more interested in how many grouse his father had bagged, and little Easton wanted to hear more about Lady Cowdray's new hospital that would be run by women—a novel idea in 1925, and one that Easton would someday pursue herself.

In the fall of 1925, John George became an American citizen. Guadalupe remained a citizen of Mexico, and the five children were made dual citizens of both Britain and the United States. Their household was truly "international," and life in San Antonio was idyllic. The big house on Russell Street was the site of parties and family gatherings. McNab cousins visited from Evanston, and Nivon cousins came from New Orleans, where Josefina and Samuel Craigie had relocated with their children in 1928.

Sometimes Guadalupe would travel to Oaxaca to see her family, often bringing back a young cousin to spend a few months in San Antonio. Her older sister Tula and husband Pablo were running the Santa Gertrudis Ranch north of Salina Cruz, and the nearby pristine beach at the foot of the cliffs was a favorite place for family reunion celebrations.

On the American "Grand Tour," the McNabs climbed Pike's Peak, where Guadalupe held her first snowball. (Photo source: Family collection.)

John George organized various adventures to introduce his wife to the landscapes of the United States; he took her to Pike's Peak and photographed her holding a snowball on top of the snowy summit; and he showed her the glamorous nightspots of New York City, as well as the famous Hudson Tunnel, which had been one of the Pearson Company's first international projects.

Just two years after the McNabs took their Grand Tour of Europe, highlighted by their weekend at Dunecht House, Lord Cowdray died unexpectedly, in his sleep, just a day before he was to receive the prestigious Aberdeen Freedom award in appreciation for all that he and Lady Cowdray had done for that Scottish city. He was seventy years old.

The event was reported around the world, and lengthy obituaries described the many accomplishments of the visionary contractor that McNab had so admired. A chapter had officially closed; John George and Guadalupe would always cherish the special time they had spent with the viscount and his family and friends in northern Scotland. Their memories of "the Chief" in Mexico were even more profound, etched forever in their hearts. His "can-do" spirit, deep curiosity, and active lifestyle well into old age would always remain inspirations to John George McNab.

When Lord Cowdray died in 1927, Britain mourned the loss of the great entrepreneur; Pearson team members like McNab knew they had lost a mentor and friend. (Photo source: Family collection.)

Fiona McNab attended the University of Texas at Austin, where
classes with the famous writer-historian J. Frank Dobie inspired her
to pursue a journalism degree. (Photo source: Family collection.)

Still robust and curious despite his own advancing age, John George
occasionally gave in to the same adventuresome spirit that had taken him
to Mexico at the turn of the century, and had lured his own father from
Scotland a generation before that. Reports of business opportunities in
Central America intrigued him, and he knew that his fluency in Spanish
and understanding of the culture could be advantageous to a potential
new venture there.

He traveled to Honduras to investigate a forestry operation, one
that his son coincidentally would pursue years later. While deep in
the jungle, he was bitten by a scorpion and had to be hospitalized for
several months before he could return to the United States. When he

finally arrived home again, he came with incredible tales of danger and survival, and with exotic gifts for the family. He brought Guadalupe an elaborate necklace and some rare cuttings for her thriving garden; a small dart set for Ian elicited shrieks of excitement, and combs inlaid with silver for his daughters earned him the hugs due a returning explorer and father.

As the McNab children moved into young adulthood, modern technology was changing their world in dramatic ways. The first transatlantic telephone call, from New York to London, was placed successfully in 1927, with considerable static on the line, and aviator Charles Lindbergh made his famous overseas flight from New York to Paris, a harbinger of the changes to come in world travel. There were also signs that marked a passing era. In 1928, General Obregón was assassinated by a religious zealot, just as he prepared to run for another term as president of Mexico. And in 1933, John George's father died in Illinois, the last of the generation that left Scotland to seek new opportunities in a new country.

Ian McNab attended Texas Military Institute in San Antonio, where he was an excellent student and a member of the football team. (Photo source: Family collection.)

Ian was enrolled in high school at Texas Military Institute, a prestigious preparatory school in San Antonio; Helena and Estella were completing degrees at the University of Texas, where Estella revealed her independent spirit when she became the first girl to "bob" her hair. Seated at the dinner table in the family home, she burst out laughing when her father simply said, "You may be excused."

As young adults, left to right, Helena, Easton, Ian, Fiona, and Estella often shared their memories of their childhoods in Mexico, marveling that their parents had sheltered them so carefully from the dangers of the revolution. (Photo source: Family collection.)

Fiona had also begun college; and her classes with the famous professor J. Frank Dobie inspired her to pursue a career in journalism. After earning her undergraduate degree, Easton went to medical school, clearly influenced by the stories her mother had told her about Lady Cowdray's interest in women's health. In 1933, she married a young medical student named Harry Gropper, and in 1935, their daughter Joan was born.

In 1940, Harry Gropper died while Easton was completing her residency in Illinois, and John George and Guadalupe brought their little granddaughter to San Antonio to live with them, following a well-established precedent in the McNab family. Just a few years before, when Helena and her husband, John Truett Patteson, decided to make a trial move to New York City to pursue their interests in the arts, they had arranged for their four-year-old daughter, Helen Patricia, to stay with the McNabs, remembering that a few decades ago John George and Guadalupe had done the same thing, sending Fiona to Illinois during the worst years of the Mexican Revolution. As the 1930s drew to a close, the big house on Russell Street echoed once more with the laughter of little children, who later, as adults, would always remember that Guadalupe possessed a special "magic," ensuring that life was fun—with a menagerie of pets, and special games that were designed to delight her grandchildren.

Estella (left) married her college sweetheart, Charles Moore, in 1935; Helena (right) had married John Truett Patteson in 1929 and moved to New York City to pursue her interest in art. (Photo source: Family collection.)

Easton McNab married Harry Gropper while still in medical school; their daughter Joan was born in 1935. (Photo source: Family collection.)

In 1937, tragedy struck the otherwise peaceful world of the McNabs. Josefina's husband, Samuel Craigie, had traveled to Mexico that summer and was returning to his family in New Orleans with a stopover to see his in-laws in San Antonio. He telephoned Guadalupe from the railroad station to say he was on his way, but he never arrived.

Police found his body not far from the Monte Vista area; he had been bludgeoned to death. The violent crime shocked the community, and the taxicab driver was arrested for murder. In New Orleans, Josefina and her two children, Albert and Millicent, were heartbroken; Guadalupe and John George were reminded again of the violence they had so wanted to escape when they immigrated to the United States. As usual, they kept the horror to themselves and were careful to protect their young grandchildren from the disturbing stories that ran in the local newspapers.

Major Ian McNab served as a Marine Corps pilot in the South Pacific during World War II. (Photo source: Family collection.)

Upon graduation from TMI, Ian enrolled at the Colorado School of Mines, planning to follow a family tradition in the oil business, but World War II brought an unexpected change in plans. With his degree barely in hand, Ian enlisted as a Marine Corps pilot in 1940. John George remembered the stories his own father had told him about his military career in India, recalling that one reason the McNab family had left Scotland was to avoid compulsory military service for their young sons. Now Ian was going willingly, passionately opposed to the atrocities going on in Europe under the leadership of a man named Adolf Hitler. When Germany's ally Japan bombed the United States naval base at Pearl Harbor in Hawaii, Americans were outraged. President Franklin Roosevelt declared war in 1941; Ian was dispatched to the South Pacific and was promoted to the rank of major not long after.

The murder of Samuel William Craigie in San Antonio was a grim reminder that violence was not limited to the nightmares of the McNab family's experiences in revolutionary Mexico. (Photo source: Family collection.)

A new generation of McNabs was shaping its own new adventures; and John George and Guadalupe watched with pride. All four daughters had married, and seven grandchildren, ranging in age from just under a year to twelve years old, brought new joy to the house in San Antonio.

Family celebrations had the same happy ambience of the Guadalajara days, filled with laughter, games, and the close ties that were being formed between the cousins.

In 1945, Ian returned from the European front, and his happy parents gave him a shiny red and chrome automobile as a welcome-home present. It was a convertible—something absolutely new in the industry—a symbol of the modern world that had somehow overtaken the past. As Ian, now as handsome as a movie star, gunned the engine to take everybody for a ride in the amazing vehicle, John George and Guadalupe laughed, wondering how the twenty-seven years since his birth in Galveston had sped by so quickly.

A new generation of McNabs brought joy to John George and Guadalupe; pictured here are their granddaughters Laura Helen Moore and Joan Gropper, with their mothers, Easton McNab Gropper and Estella McNab Moore, circa 1938. (Photo source: Family collection.)

The next few years seemed to move at the same fast pace. Four more grandchildren had joined the clan; now a band of eleven cousins explored the huge family home, delighting in the secret hiding places they created under the massive staircase and in the treasures they discovered that linked them to their not-so-distant past in Mexico. A stuffed alligator and a jaguar rug were especially thrilling finds, certain evidence that

Guadalupe loved her gardens; roses had been a constant in
Oaxaca, Chihuahua, Tampico, Guadalajara, and, finally,
San Antonio. (Photo source: Family collection.)

John George McNab's youth had been filled with daring exploits. Little
did they know that alligators and jaguars were not nearly as dangerous
as the real challenges of revolution and murder had been.

San Juanito Ranch was just outside San Antonio, a hub of adventure for
increasing numbers of McNab grandchildren. (Photo source: Family collection.)

The Feast of St. John remained a constant in the McNab family; each year Guadalupe supervised the preparation of the meal that had become the very essence of celebration—chicken tamales, with mole and raisins mixed into the *masa,* wrapped in banana leaves that now grew in the yard. John George and his grandchildren were in charge of shelling the pecans that would eventually be transformed into the pecan pies their grandmother baked for this special occasion, and of trips to the nearby ranch, just outside the city limits of San Antonio, to gather the nuts; feeding the new lambs with a baby bottle was always an adventure.

Guadalupe and John George had made sure that the Russell Street house was large enough to comfortably accommodate all of their children and grandchildren as the family expanded. Its halls echoed with laughter; its library was a source of both information and great games of hide-and-go-seek; its gardens offered secret places to build forts and playhouses, and wonderful smells emanated from the bustling kitchen. Helena, Estella, Fiona, and Easton all had children old enough to romp together, inventing adventures that they would cherish forever. Their mothers smiled at the exuberant gang of cousins, understanding that these deep bonds of family were the greatest gift possible.

Roses filled the side yard, and as the years passed, they became more resplendent. Their deep red blossoms were reminders of earlier days in Mexico, of Guadalupe's own patron saint, and of the kneeling pillows made for a wedding at the turn of the century, uniting thistles and roses. Just as the rose garden on Russell Street had matured, producing more variations each year, Guadalupe's beauty also deepened. Her children and grandchildren seemed to know that although John George was the family's patriarch, Guadalupe was "secretly in charge."

When Guadalupe Nivon McNab became ill in 1953, her symptoms were vague—loss of appetite, fatigue, and unexplained weight loss despite the feasts she continued to oversee. Dramatic gray streaks had added character to her thick dark hair, and she still turned heads when

Although Helena McNab Patteson lived the farthest away, in New York, with her husband and three daughters, she often visited San Antonio so the increasing number of grandchildren could share family adventures. (Photo source: Family collection.)

she moved through a room with her elegant grace. When she died of stomach cancer the following year, she was sixty-nine years old. John George was devastated; his five children and their expanded families circled around him in support as he mustered his Scottish traits of privacy and reserve to thank the large number of friends and family that called on him to offer their condolences.

The funeral was held in San Fernando Cathedral, San Antonio's oldest church, located in downtown's Main Plaza. Hundreds of candles created a magical luminescence that reminded John George of the beautiful cathedral in Oaxaca where he had joined his life with Guadalupe's in 1904. Wreaths of red roses adorned the basilica and

Always a wonderful storyteller, John George often gathered his grandchildren
for tales of adventure in Mexico; pictured here are Maggie and namesake
John George "Sandy" McNab. (Photo source: Family collection.)

covered the coffin. His eyes misted as he silently said good-bye, reciting
the words of John Keats's great love poem, "Now a soft kiss—aye, by
that kiss, I vow an endless bliss."

She was buried in City Cemetery #1, where John George made sure
the McNab family plot was planted with more roses and that the new
tombstone would endure for centuries to come.

The idea of living in the big house without Guadalupe was
incomprehensible to him; he sold the Russell Street home and moved in
with Estella and her family. He had always adored his second daughter,
admiring her independent spirit even when she did things as shocking
as bobbing her hair without permission. She had fallen in love with,
and married, Charles Monroe Moore while he was in pharmacy school
at the University of Texas, and McNab liked and respected his son-in-
law. Now established as a successful pharmacist in San Antonio, Moore
was delighted when his wife told him that their household was about to
expand; he welcomed his father-in-law with open arms.

The Moores had one child, a beautiful daughter named Laura Helen, who was a freshman in college when Guadalupe died. Laura had spent many days and nights with her grandparents, and, as an only child, she cherished the special relationship she had with them both. Now she would have a unique opportunity to spend some very special years with her *"Papá,"* appreciating his unique capacity for listening and the quiet wisdom he shared with her on topics that ranged from business to politics to the way young ladies should behave in the 1950s.

Ian also lived in San Antonio, with his wife and two small children. Their son, named John George McNab in honor of his grandfather and great-grandfather, was three years old, and their baby daughter, Maggie, was just eighteen months old when Guadalupe died. Fiona and her growing family lived in nearby Pasadena, Texas; Helena and her husband and children lived in New York, and Easton had remarried and lived with her family in Illinois, where she was practicing medicine.

The next few years brought three more grandchildren, and each new life was a poignant sign that the family still was linked to its ancestors in deep and powerful ways. Some had Guadalupe's dark eyes and thick chestnut hair, reminders of the Nivon and Fuentes families of France and Mexico; others had blue eyes and sandy-blond hair, like the Scottish McNabs that went back so many generations.

John George had moved his collection of classic literature, history, and engineering texts into the library of the Moore house, and on its back patio, overlooking a rose garden, John George had built a state-of-the-art telescope.

When he looked up at the stars through the telescope's lens, he imagined Guadalupe among them, the brightest star of all. When the famous comet of 1957 blazed across the skies, he gathered his San Antonio–based grandchildren for a night of stargazing, and together they watched the fiery path of the comet.

He held his six-year-old namesake on his lap and told the little clan about their extraordinary grandmother and their adventures together in Mexico, and of the great love they had shared. As the light faded in the night sky, the youngest children understood that the story was over and

John George McNab always loved the independent spirit of his
daughter Estella; he encountered the same traits in his granddaughter,
Laura Helen Moore. (Photo source: Family collection.)

that it was time for bed. The older ones had more questions about the
grandmother they remembered so well, and about the adventures that
had taken place long ago in a distant land. John George, now eighty-six
years old, softly tousled his grandson's sandy-brown hair and marveled
at the little cleft in his chin, so like his own. And as he looked at his
granddaughters, he saw Guadalupe's dark eyes and chestnut hair. He
felt a deep confidence that the story would never end.

In 1960, John George McNab died peacefully, a victim of
pneumonia. He was eighty-nine years old; surrounded by his family,
he was serene, perhaps sensing that he would soon be reunited with

his beloved Guadalupe. Just a few days before, as he slipped in and out of dreams, he had quoted his favorite poet of all, Robert Burns, softly reciting a few verses that reminded his children of the long life he had lived. They had heard him recite the poem at every celebration of his birthday; they had sung it together as each new year began, and they understood its power.

The words, in ancient brogue, conjured up the heroic journey, from moors to jungles and mountains, where a Scottish "thistle" and a Mexican "rose" created the family that now tenderly circled its patriarch's bed. And they vowed that the story would never be forgotten.

Should auld acquaintance be forgot
And never brought to mind?
Should auld acquaintance be forgot
And auld lang syne!

We twa hae paidl'd in the burn,
Frae morning sun till dine;
But seas between us braid hae roar'd
Sin auld lang syne.

For auld lang syne, my dear,
For auld lang syne.
We'll tak a cup o' kindness yet,
For auld lang syne.

John George McNab was courageous and sturdy like the hearty thistles in his native Scotland. Guadalupe Fuentes Nivon was both tender and strong, like the red roses that grew in her gardens in Mexico and Texas. (Photo source: Family collection.)

Notes

Chapter 1: A Fiery Start

Reference to Mexican peasants' reaction to Halley's Comet: Anita Brenner and George R. Leighton, *The Wind that Swept Mexico* (Austin: University of Texas Press, 1943), 18.

Reference to German financier Hugo Scherer: Ibid., 16.

Reference to M. de Bucareli sending an engineer to the Isthmus: *Francie B. Chassen-Lopez, From Liberal to Revolutionary Oaxaca* (University Park: Pennsylvania State University Press, 2004).

Reference to President Santa Anna's concession to Gaetano Moro: Ibid.

Reference to Eagle Pass, Texas, Courthouse costing $20,489 to build: "Maverick County Courthouses," Texas Escapes online magazine; The Handbook of Texas Online.

References to rancher P. W. Thomson in Eagle Pass, Texas: *Southwestern Reporter*, 49 (Eagle Pass Public Library); timeline of Eagle Pass history, Eagle Pass Library, and McNab family documents.

Chapter 2: Mists and Moors

Reference to Mac-an-Abba (Son of the Abbott): Genealogy research conducted by Easton McNab Crawford; John McNab, "The Clan MacNab: A Short Sketch" (Edinburgh, Scotland: The Clan MacNab Association, Internet archive, 1907).

Reference to land records in Scotland: Ibid.

References to Sir Thomas Poe and Emperor Jahangir: "British East India Company," Wikipedia Free Encyclopedia Online.

References to the Sepoy Mutiny: Ibid.; interviews with British military historian Robin Cross.

References to Colonel James Anderson and Andrew Carnegie: "Andrew Carnegie Biography," Wikipedia Free Encyclopedia Online.

References to Major Robert MacNab: John McNab, "The Clan MacNab: A Short Sketch" (Edinburgh, Scotland: The Clan MacNab Association, Internet archive, 1907); Honorable Nelson King, "Soldier, Statesman, and Freemason" (Toronto: self-published, 2009).

References to Sir Weetman Pearson's biographical information: Original documents (Wroughton, United Kingdom: Pearson Archive, Science Museum Library); "Sir Weetman Pearson," Wikipedia Free Encyclopedia Online.

References to McNab family's transatlantic crossing: "The Great Transatlantic Liners," Maritime Archives & Library; "Crossing the Atlantic," New York Times, July 23, 1880; McNab family letters.

Chapter 3: Castles and Kings

References to "The Lion in Love": "Correspondence de Madame de Sévigné," Texte établi, présenté et annoté par Roger Duchêne. (Paris: Bibliothèque de la Pléiade); "The Lion in Love," Jean de la Fontaine, accessible at readbookonline.net; Wikipedia Free Encyclopedia Online.

References to Napoleon in Valence: Bourrienne, Memoirs of Napoleon Bonaparte (New York: Charles Scribners Sons, 1891).

References to Compagnie Franco-Mexicaine: "Le Mirage de l'Eldorado: 1833: La Colonisation de Jicaltepec, Veracruz," published by mexicoaccueil.com; "Jicaltepec: Chroniqe d'un village francais au Mexique," pour Jean-Christophe Demard, Paris.

References to letters from French immigrants regarding their voyages to Mexico: Ibid.

References to yellow fever epidemic in Vera Cruz: Multiple sources, including Frederick A. Ober, *Travels in Mexico* (Boston: Estes and Lauriat, 1884).

Reference to staircase of fifty-seven steps at Pyramid of Papantla: Ibid.

Reference to letter from French Foreign Minister Mole: Robert Spence Robertson, "French Intervention in Mexico in 1838," *The Hispanic American Historical Review*, 24, No. 2 (May 1944), Duke University Press; "French Blockade of Veracruz: 1838," Wikipedia Free Encyclopedia Online.

References to cochineal insect and natural dye process: Multiple sources, including interviews by Catherine Nixon Cooke with traditional dye-makers in Oaxaca; Museo Textil de Oaxaca (Alejandro de Avila, director); El Carocol Púrpura: Una Tradición Milenaria en Oaxaca," Marta Turok, secretaria de Educación Pública (publisher), 1988.

References to President Santa Anna's sale of Mexican land to the United States in 1853: Enrique Krauze, *Mexico: Biography of Power* (New York: HarperCollins, 1997).

Chapter 4: Déjà Vu

References to natural dye production in mid-1800s: Interviews with Bulamaro Pérez Mendoza (natural dye producer), by Catherine Nixon Cooke, Teotitlán, Oaxaca, Mexico, October 2009; "El Carocol Púrpura:

Una Tradición Milenaria en Oaxaca," Marta Turok, secretaria de educación pública (publisher), 1988.

References to bonds held by the Duc de Morny: Nancy N. Barker, "The French Legation in Mexico," copyright 1974, Society for French Historical Studies.

References to matriarchal society in Oaxaca: Multiple sources including magazines and research materials archived in the Palacio Municipal de Tehuantepec Library, Tehuantepec, Oaxaca, Mexico.

References to Juana Catarina Romero's biography: Ibid.; Francie R. Chassen, "Juana Catarina Romero: Cacica porfiriana," *Calenda Magazine*, May 2003, University of Kentucky; "Mercado de Tehuantepec," Mexican Bureau of Education (AGN), 1909; Gustavo Toledo Morales, "Juana Cata Romero," unedited manuscript, copies of documents from the personal archive of Doña Juana C. Romero, donated to the Palacio Municipal de Tehuantepec Library by Doña Elena Evangelina Romero Cartas.

References to reforms made by Maximilian while Emperor of Mexico: Enrique Krauze, *Mexico: Biography of Power* (New York: HarperCollins, 1997).

References to biographical facts about Benito Juárez and Porfirio Díaz: Ibid., and multiple publications listed in the bibliography.

References to the Chatino revolt/"War of the Pants": Francie R. Chassen-Lopez, *From Liberal to Revolutionary Oaxaca* (University Park: Pennsylvania State University Press, 2004); James B. Greenberg, *Blood Ties: Life and Violence in Rural Mexico* (Tucson: University of Arizona Press, 1989).

Chapter 5: The Thistle and the Rose

References to railroad detour to accommodate President Díaz: María de los Angeles Cajigas, "Porfirio Díaz y Juana Cata," *Calenda Magazine*, May 2003; Gustavo Toledo Morales, "Juana Cata Romero," unedited manuscript (both sources located in the Palacio Municipal de Tehuantepec Library, Tehuantepec, Oaxaca, Mexico); Enrique Krauze, *Mexico: Biography of Power* (New York: HarperCollins, 1997).

References to Sir Weetman Pearson's speech at Tehuantepec Railroad Inauguration: Original document/texts, Pearson Archives, Science Museum Library, Wroughton, United Kingdom.

References to port activity resulting from new railroad: Ibid.

References to quotes by Sir Weetman Pearson: Ibid.

References to $80 million investment by El Aguila: Ibid.

References to production volume of El Potrero #4 oil well: Ibid., and Paul Garner, PhD, "Weetman Pearson and Mexican National Development, 1889-1919" (United Kingdom: University of Leeds, 2008); Lisa Bud Frierman, Andrew Godley, and Judith Vale, "Weetman Pearson in Mexico and the Emergence of a British Oil Major, 1901-1919" (United Kingdom: Centre for International Business History, University of Reading Business School, 2007).

References to petroleum engineer Everette de Golyer: Ibid., and Wikipedia Free Encyclopedia Online.

Chapter 6: The Red-Haired Angel

References to net worth/landholdings of Terrazas-Creel Family: Anita Brenner and George Leighton *The Wind that Swept Mexico* (Austin: University of Texas Press, 1943); Stafford Youkey, "Enrique Creel

Cuilty," Historical Text Archive (historicaltextarchive.com); Wikipedia Free Encyclopedia Online.

References to Pearson's invention of the submarine pipeline: Original documents and letters, Pearson Archive, Science Museum Library, Wroughton, United Kingdom.

References to Eagle Oil contracts: Ibid.; Lisa Bud Frierman, Andrew Godley, and Judith Vale, "Weetman Pearson in Mexico and the Emergence of a British Oil Major, 1901-1919," (Reading, United Kingdom: Centre for International Business History, University of Reading Business School).

References to telegram from General Huerta to US President Taft: Anita Brenner and George Leighton, *The Wind that Swept Mexico* (Austin: University of Texas Press, 1943); Enrique Krauze, *Mexico: Biography of Power* (New York: HarperCollins, 1997).

References to Pearson family personal information: Original documents, Pearson Archives, Science Museum Library, Wroughton, United Kingdom.

Chapter 7: Precarious Times

References to architecture of Tampico in the eighteenth and early nineteenth century: Frederick A. Ober, *Travels in Mexico* (Boston: Estes and Lauriat, 1884).

References to Tampico's electric tram system: Ibid.

References to Iturbide's escape from Mexico: Original documents and Iturbide letter to US secretary of state (Wroughton, United Kingdom: Pearson Archive, Science Museum Library).

References to President Carranza's plan for the oil industry: Enrique Krauze, *Mexico: Biography of Power* (New York: HarperCollins, 1997).

References to President Wilson's appeal to the Mexicans: Ibid.

Chapter 8: Chaos and Courage

References to the Hurricane of 1915 in Galveston, Texas: Wikipedia Free Encyclopedia Online.

References to Dominican Sisters in Galveston: Interviews conducted by Catherine Nixon Cooke; original documents in the Dominican Archive, Houston, Texas; Sheila Hackett, OP, *Dominican Women in Texas* (Houston: Sacred Heart Convent of Houston, 1986).

References to Interim President Carranza's march to Querétaro: Enrique Krauze, *Mexico: Biography of Power* (New York: HarperCollins, 1997).

References to Lord Cowdray's war activities in England: Original documents, Pearson Archive, Science Museum Library, Wroughton, United Kingdom.

References to 1917 Constitutional Convention: Enrique Krauze, *Mexico: Biography of Power* (New York: HarperCollins, 1997).

Reference to Sir Thomas Hohler's memo regarding General Peláez: Original document, Pearson Archive, Science Museum Library, Wroughton, United Kingdom; Enrique Krauze, *Mexico: Biography of Power* (New York: HarperCollins, 1997).

Chapter 9: Beginnings and Endings

References to Lord Cowdray's land holdings in Mexico: Original documents, Pearson Archives, Science Museum Library, Wroughton, United Kingdom.

References to oil production levels in Mexico's "Golden Lane": Lisa Bud Frierman, Andrew Godley, and Judith Vale, "Weetman Pearson in Mexico and the Emergence of a British Oil Major, 1889-1919" (United Kingdom: Centre for International Business History, University of Reading Business School, 2007).

References to Calouste Gulbenkian as the Armenian "Mr. Five Percent": Ibid.

References to Lord Cowdray family personal information: Original documents, Pearson Archive, Science Museum Library, Wroughton, United Kingdom.

References to assassination of Emiliano Zapata: Enrique Krauze, *Mexico: Biography of Power*, (New York: HarperCollins, 1997).

Chapter 10: Reunion

References to assassination of President Carranza: New York Times, May 27, 1920; Wikipedia Free Encyclopedia Online.

References to "The Five Chapter Plan": Original documents and letters, Pearson Archive, Science Museum Library, Wroughton, United Kingdom.

References to history of Studebaker Automobile Company: Stephen Longstreet, *A Century on Wheels: The Story of Studebaker* (New York: Henry Holt, 1952); "Studebaker," Wikipedia Free Online Encyclopedia.

References to British Consul Percy Holmes in Mexico: New York Times, May 9, 1914, and May 21, 1914; William Brownlee Davis, M.D., "Experiences and Observations of an American Consular Officer During the Recent Mexican Revolutions," (Los Angeles: published by the author/Wayside Press, 1920).

References to the US Senate investigations of "The Mexican Situation": Ibid.

Chapter 11: Revelations

References to Lord and Lady Cowdray: Original documents, Pearson Archive, Science Museum Library, Wroughton, United Kingdom; personal documents in the McNab Family collection.

References to the assassination of President Obregón: Enrique Krauze, *Mexico: Biography of Power* (New York: HarperCollins, 1997).

Bibliography

Primary Sources
Original Manuscripts, Personal Papers, Photograph Collections

1. *Nivon-McNab Family History.* Teresa Van Hoy, PhD, commissioned by Laura Helen Moore Brusenhan and John George ("Sandy") McNab, 2006.
2. Nivon-McNab Family scrapbooks, notes, and photographs. Collection of Estella McNab Moore and Laura Helen Moore Brusenhan.
   Collection of Ian McNab and John George McNab III.
   Collection of Millicent Antelma Gertrudis Craigie Keck.
3. Family surveys. Catherine Nixon Cooke; received from Easton McNab Crawford, Joan Gropper Crawford Mattson, Mary Isabel "Ibby" Crawford, Laura Helen Moore Brusenhan, John George "Sandy" McNab, Judith "Judy" Virginia Grafius Griffith, and Elizabeth "Betty" Isabel Grafius Moore, 2007-8.
4. *The Pearson Archive.* Science Museum Library, Wroughton, United Kingdom; research access by Catherine Nixon Cooke to papers, letters, photographs, February 2009.
5. *The Sacred Heart Academy Archive.* Dominican Sisters of Houston, Houston, Texas; research access by Catherine Nixon Cooke to papers, school records, photographs, February 2009.
6. *Palacio Municipal de Tehuantepec Archive.* Tehuantepec, Oaxaca, Mexico; research access by Catherine Nixon Cooke to manuscripts, articles, photographs, October 2009.
7. *Eagle Pass Public Library.* Eagle Pass, Texas; research access by Catherine Nixon Cooke to documents about the history of the P. W. Thomson Ranch.

8. *"Weetman Pearson and Mexican National Development, 1889-1919."* Paul Garner, PhD, University of Leeds, United Kingdom, 2008.
9. *"Weetman Pearson in Mexico and the Emergence of a British Oil Major, 1901–1919."* Lisa Bud Frierman, Andrew Godley, and Judith Vale, Centre for International Business History, University of Reading Business School, United Kingdom, 2007.

Interviews

1. Moore, Estella McNab. Conducted and recorded by Laura Moore Brusenhan and Sandy McNab in San Antonio, 2001, *family history and personal remembrances.*
2. Crawford, Easton McNab. Conducted by Mary Isabel "Ibby" Crawford and the author, July 2007, *family history and personal remembrances.*
3. Nivon, Alejandro. Conducted by the author, New York City, August 2007, *family history and personal remembrances.*
4. Grossman, Shirley Fleishman. Conducted by the author, San Antonio, Texas, 2008, *anecdotes about life in Tampico, Mexico, during the oil boom.*
5. Longoria, Ricardo and Cheri. Conducted by the author, San Antonio, Texas, 2008, *anecdotes about life in Mexico during the Mexican Revolution.*
6. Hanel, Sister Mary Magdalene. Director of Archives, Dominican Sisters of Houston, conducted by the author, Houston, Texas, January 2009, *history and anecdotes about Sacred Heart Academy in Galveston, Texas.*
7. Rodriguez, Raul. Former Chairman, North American Development Bank, conducted by the author, San Antonio, Texas, March 2009, *history and anecdotes about politics and business in Mexico.*
8. Malo, Gabriela Nivon. Conducted by the author, San Antonio, Texas, June 2009, *family history and anecdotes.*

9. Jackson, George O. Jr. Conducted by the author, Austin, Texas, October 2009, *descriptions and photographs of traditional feast days of San Juan and patron saint, La Virgen de Guadalupe, in Mexico.*

10. *Mendoza,* Bulamaro Perez. Conducted by the author, Teotitlán, Oaxaca, Mexico, October 2009, *history and details of anil and cochineal natural dye industry in Mexico.*

11. Villalobos, Dr. Samuel. Director, Biblioteca Pública Municipal, Palacio Municipal de Tehuantepec, conducted by the author, Tehuantepec, Oaxaca, Mexico, October 2009, *history and anecdotes about Juana Catarina Romero, entrepreneurial women of Oaxaca, and the Petriz family of Tehuantepec.*

12. Langner, Arnoldo Nivon. Conducted by the author, Tapanatepec, Oaxaca, Mexico, October 2009, *Nivon family history and anecdotes about the hacienda era in southern Mexico.*

13. Keck, Millicent Antelma Gertrudis Craigie. Conducted by the author, Savannah, Georgia, May 2010, *Nivon family history and details of life in Salina Cruz, Mexico from 1918 to 1928; access to extensive photograph collection.*

Publications

Van Hoy, Teresa. A Social History of Mexico's Railroads. Lanham, MD: Rowman & Littlefield, 2008.

Bedford, Sybille. A Visit to Don Octovio: A Traveller's Tale from Mexico. New York: Counterpoint, 1953.

Clendenen, Clarence C. Blood on the Border. London: Macmillan, 1969.

McNab, John. "The Clan MacNab: A Short Sketch," Edinburgh, Scotland: The Clan McNab Association, 1907.

Duchêne, Roger. Correspondence de Madame Sévigné, (three volumes). Paris: Bibliothèque de la Pléiade.

Hackett, Sheila, OP. Dominican Women in Texas. Sacred Heart Convent of Houston, Texas, 1986.

Turok, Marta. El Caracol Púrpura: Una Tradición Milenaria en Oaxaca. Mexican Department of Public Education, Mexico, 1988.

Reyes, Bernardo. El General Porfirio Díaz, D. J. Ballesca y Compañía, Sucesores, Editores, México, 1903.

El Zapoteco, Número 5, September—October 2005.

Davis, William Brownlee, MD. Experiences and Observances of an American Consular Officer during the Recent Mexican Revolutions. Los Angeles: Wayside Press, 1920.

Robertson, Robert Spence. "French Intervention in Mexico in 1838." *The Hispanic American Historical Review,* 24, No. 2, Duke University, 1944.

Barker, Nancy N. The French Legation in Mexico. Society for French Historical Studies, 1974.

Chassen-Lopez, Francie R. From Liberal to Revolutionary Oaxaca. **University Park:** Pennsylvania State University Press, 2004.

Johnson, David Nathan. Madero in Texas. San Antonio, TX: Corona, 2001.

Bourricane. Memoirs of Napoleon Bonaparte. New York: Charles Scribner's Sons, 1891.

Gonzales, Michael J. The Mexican Revolution 1910–1940. Albuquerque: University of New Mexico Press, 2002.

Krauze, Enrique. Mexico: Biography of Power. New York: HarperCollins, 1997.

The New York Times: "Crossing the Atlantic," July 23, 1880; "Conference Begins With Broad Scope and All Sides Hopeful," May 21, 1914; "Tried to Massacre American Colony," January 20, 1920; "Herrera Men Murders," May 23, 1920; "Carranza's Aides Tell of Murder in the Mountains," May 25, 1920; "Herrera Gives Up: Is Taken to Mexico City," May 26, 1920.

Wright, Marie Robinson. Picturesque Mexico. Philadelphia: J. B. Lippincott, 1897.

Cajigas, María de los Angeles. "Porfirio Díaz y Juana Cata," *Calenda Magazine*, Oaxaca, Mexico, May 2003.

Martinez, Melesio Ortega. Reseña Histórica de Tehuantepec. Biblioteca Pública Municipál, Tehuantepec, Oaxaca, Mexico, 1998.

Romo, David Dorado. Ringside Seat to A Revolution. El Paso, TX: Cinco Puntos Press, 2005.

King, Hon. Nelson. Soldier, Statesman, and Freemason. Toronto, Canada: Self-published, 2009.

Ober, Frederick A. Travels in Mexico. Boston: Estes and Lauriat, 1884.

McLyn, Frank. Villa and Zapata. New York: Carrol & Graf, 2000.

Brenner, Anita, and George R. Leighton. The Wind that Swept Mexico. Austin: University of Texas Press, 1943.

Garcia, Roberto Williams. Yo Nací con la Luna de Plata. Veracruz, Mexico: Costa-Amic Editores, 1979.

Parkinson, Roger. Zapata. New York: Stein and Day, 1975.

Electronic Sources

Ancestry.com (genealogy research and data).

Archives.com (genealogy research and public records).

The Handbook of Texas Online (history of Eagle Pass, Texas).

Historicaltextarchive.com (*"Enrique Creel Cuilty,"* Stafford Youkey)

Intelius.com (public records)
"Le Mirage de l'Eldorado: 1833: La Colonisation de Jicaltepec, Veracruz," Mexicoaccueil.com.

Texas Escapes Online Magazine (*"Maverick County Courthouses"*).

Wikipedia Free Encyclopedia Online.

Index

Mexico
advertisement (1833) of potential in,
44*ph*
assassination of Carranza in
Tlaxcalatongo (Puebla), 188–91
attack of US consul in Guadalajara
(Mexico), 199–200
Banco Nacional de México
(Tehuantepec), 68
Catedrál Metropolitana (Mexico
City), 64
cholera epidemic in Atencingo, 49
civil war of 1860, 56
connecting east and west coast of, 7–9,
37*ph*. *see also* Tehuantepec Railroad
Constitution in Querétaro in 1917,
138
Constitutional Convention (1917),
138, 151, 152, 153, 153*ph*
creating national oil industry, 140–41
discovery of oil in, xi
in dye production, 53–55
dye production in, 59–61, 61*ph*, 65,
67–68. *see also* cochineal insect
French laborers in, 43–44
Germany proposes alliance (WWI)
with, 154–55
integration of workers along US
border, 110
Lerdo laws (1856), 65–66
Malatengo Canyon, 95
modernization of Mexico, 1–3
oil and mineral nationalized, 152,
159, 159*ph*
oil development on Isthmus of
Tehuantepec, 89–93, 99, 102, 107,
108*ph*
oil exploration suspended in, 139
oil fields in turmoil in, 156, 156*ph*,
186
oil output of, 167
oil pipelines in, 122, 159, 167
oil production in, 175
oil production in Tampico, 131, 168
Palacio Nacional (Tehuantepec), 74
patron saint of, 76, 85, 132, 170,
170*ph*, 172–74

revolutionary activity in. *see*
revolutionary activity
ruins of Papantla, 47*ph*
selling land to United States, 55, 56
yellow fever in Veracruz, 46–47
Mexico City
"bandit" armies enter, 138
Catedrál Metropolitana in, 64
Gran Canal, 3, 36–38
railroad to Veracruz from, 9, 10*ph*
violence from revolutionary activity
in, 118, 118*ph*
Minatitlán (Mexico), 99, 159
Miracle of Guadalupe, 170, 170*ph*, 173.
see also Virgin of Guadalupe
Mole, Foreign Minister, 49
Monroe Doctrine, 63
Moore, Charles Monroe, 223, 230
Moore, Estella McNab (wife of Charles
Monroe Moore). *see* McNab, Estella
(daughter of John George McNab)
Moore, Laura Helen (granddaughter of
John George McNab), ix, x, 182, 204,
226*ph*, 231–32, 232, 232*ph*
Morelos (Mexico), 158, 177–79
Morny, duc de, 62
Moro, Gaetano, 7–8
Mory, Petrona, 71
motor vehicles, 193*ph*
beginning era in Mexico of, 193–95
convertible automobiles, 226
Mount Colima (volcano), 1–2, 1*ph*, 113,
201
Mount Orizaba (volcano), 46, 201
M.S. Novara (ship), 64

N
Napoleon, 42
Napoleon III, Emperor of France, 61–62,
62, 68–69
National Mexican Company of Dynamite
and Explosives, 109
National Railways of Mexico, 100, 101
nationalization of oil and minerals
(Mexico), 152, 159, 159*ph*
native culture, in Oaxaca, 66
New Orleans, 11, 71, 129, 195, 206

261

New York City (NYC), Hudson Tunnel, 218

New York Times
   on assassination of Carranza, 186, 188–91
   on attack of US consul in Guadalajara (Mexico), 199
   on Pancho Villa, 116
   Pearson in, 35

Niddrin, William, 24

Nivon, Anastacia Fuentes de (grandmother of Guadalupe Fuentes Nivon), 74*ph*
   about, 50
   after death of husband, 77, 80
   celebrating fiftieth birthday of husband in France, 59
   children of, 55–56
   at coronation of Emperor Ferdinand Maximilian, 64
   invitation to John George McNab to Santa Yfigenia, 14, 17*ph*
   involvement in land disputes, 65–66
   marriage of, 51–52
   meeting Jean Antoine Nivon, 40
   at wedding of Guadalupe Fuentes Nivon, 86

Nivon, Antoine. *see* Nivon, Jean Antoine "Don Antonio" (grandfather of Guadalupe Fuentes Nivon)

Nivon, Antonio (son of Jean Antoine Nivon "Don Antonio"), 56, 59, 65

Nivon, Carlos, 77

Nivon, Delfina (daughter of Jean Antoine Nivon "Don Antonio"), 59

Nivon, Don Antonio. *see* Nivon, Jean Antoine "Don Antonio" (grandfather of Guadalupe Fuentes Nivon)

Nivon, Féderico (father of Guadalupe Fuentes Nivon), 76*ph*
   about, 17
   birth of, 56
   children of, 76–77
   education of, 74
   escorts Guadalupe Fuentes Nivon to ball, 5
   interest in farming techniques, 59

   marriage of, 75
   at wedding of daughter Guadalupe, 87

Nivon, Gertrudis (mother of Guadalupe Fuentes Nivon), 17, 75*ph*, 76–77, 76*ph*, 86

Nivon, Gertrudis "Tula" (sister of Guadalupe Fuentes Nivon), 58, 88, 89*ph*, 217*ph*, 218

Nivon, Guadalupe Fuentes (wife of John George McNab), 7*ph*, 86*ph*, 127*ph*, 132*ph*, 163*ph*, 172*ph*, 183*ph*, 234*ph*
   about, xi
   birth of, 76
   birthdays celebrations of, 85, 172–73, 175, 198–99
   Body reunion with family of, 177
   child in Illinois, 149, 149*ph*, 150, 160, 160–61, 165
   children celebrating holidays, 164
   children in adulthood, 221–26
   children in Texas, 145–49, 156–58, 160
   children of, 92, 101, 113, 115, 128, 132*ph*, 141–42, 165–66
   death of, 228–30
   death of husband, 232–33
   description of, xx, xxii, 58
   encounter with Pancho Villa, 117
   engagement of, 83
   favorite flower of, 170
   fears for husband's life, 127
   Feast of St. John celebrations, 131–33, 185, 228
   gardens of, 227, 227*ph*, 228
   grandchildren of, ix, 18, 144, 182, 204, 222, 223, 223*ph*, 226–28, 226*ph*, 227*ph*, 229*ph*, 230*ph*, 231–32
   granddaughter on, 144
   in Guadalajara, 194*ph*, 195*ph*
   heritage of, 80
   home in Guadalajara, 183–85, 195
   home in northern Mexico, 115–16, 115*ph*
   home in San Antonio, 208–9, 208*ph*, 217–18, 228
   home in Santa Cruz, 87, 87*ph*, 98, 99

University of Wisconsin, 36
Urseline Academy, at Our Lady of the
Lake University, 209

V

Van Hoy, Teresa, x, xii
vanilla trade, 47–48
Veracruz (Mexico)
  Carranza sets up government in,
    138–39
  emigrants arriving in, 46, 46*ph*, 48–49
  foreign military occupation of, 56
  French laborers in, 43–44
  harbor project, 3, 38
  malaria in, 56
  railroad to Mexico City from, 9, 10*ph*
  yellow fever in, 46–47, 56
Veracruz and Isthmian Railway, 94
Vespucius, Americus, 129
Victoria, Queen, 19, 22, 25, 64
Victoria Falls (Africa), 22
Viking publishing group, 175
Villa, Francisco "Pancho," 116*ph*
  about, 106
  defeat by Carranistas of, 178
  entering Mexico City with "bandit"
    army, 138, 139*ph*
  Iturbide hiding from, 135–36
  meeting with John George McNab,
    116–19, 118*ph*, 138
  in northern Mexico, 106, 116–17
  not recognizing Victoriano Huerta's
    government, 134
  recharging his revolutionary forces,
    124
  relationship with Carranza, 187
  revolutionary activity in northern
    Mexico, 116–17
  wages war against Carranza regime,
    158
"La Villa Rica de la Vera Cruz," 46
La Virgen Morena (the Dark Virgin),
  173–74, 173*ph*
Virgin of Guadalupe, 76, 85, 170, 170*ph*,
  172–73

W

Wallace, Robert, 11
Walsh, Mrs., at American School
  (Guadalajara), 185
"The War of the Pants," 80
Waters Pierce, Pearson negotiating
  agreement to refine and ship crude of,
  99
White Star Line, 32, 123
Whitehall Petroleum Company Ltd., 175
Wickersham, George W., 100
Wilson, James, 22
Wilson, Woodrow, 134–37, 141, 155
women, in native culture of Oaxaca, 66
Woolrich, Carlos, 80
World War I (WWI)
  Air Board in Great Britain during,
    151, 153
  beginning of, 126
  blockade of German ports by Great
    Britain during, 171
  dispensation from military service of
    John George McNab during, 166,
    166*ph*
  efforts by Pearson, 151
  end of, 171–72
  Germany proposes alliance with
    Mexico, 154–55
  oil demand during, 167
World War II (WWII)
  bombing of Pearl Harbor, 225
  Ian McNab's military service during,
    224–26
Wroughton (Great Britain), Pearson
  Archive at Science Museum Library,
  153

X

Xalapa, French laborers in, 44

Y

yellow fever
  about steamship *Antilian*, 147
  in Veracruz, 46–47, 56
Ypiranga (ship), 120